OCR AS Computer Science (H046)

Revision Notes

Joe Harris

First published 2016.

ISBN-13: 978-1548705398
ISBN-10: 154870539X
Version 2.1

With thanks to Dan Wright from Suffolk One for letting me use some of his awesome diagrams!

Spot any errors? Have any complaints or questions?
@JoeHarrisUK
joeh1999@live.com

Contents

The processor is designed to follow millions of instructions per second in order to produce useful outputs. These include sorting, searching, calculations, logical decisions and controlling input/output devices.

Arithmetic and Logic Unit (ALU):

- Carries out all calculations (fixed/floating point arithmetic and logical comparisons)
- The range of calculations it can perform is known as its **instruction set**
- Acts as a gateway to the processor; all inputs and outputs pass through the ALU before being directed to other parts of the processor/computer system

Control Unit (CU):

- Controlled by a clock which produces electrical pulses to synchronise the activity of the parts of the CPU
- Controls the movement of data in the CPU (e.g. fetching instructions or data from main memory)
- Manages the execution of instructions by synchronising parts of the CPU
- Sends control signals to other parts of the computer
- Controls the **fetch, decode, execute cycle** (see page 5)

Special purpose registers:

- Extremely fast memory
- Used to temporarily store data and addresses that move between the CPU and main memory (RAM) and are used by the CPU for the execution of instructions

  Program Counter (PC):

    o Controls the <u>order</u> in which instructions are retrieved and executed
    o Holds the main memory address of the **next instruction** to be fetched, decoded and executed
    o Once this instruction has been fetched, the PC is incremented to point to the address of the next instruction in the queue
    o Some instructions may modify the next address held in the PC; these are known as **jump instructions** and are used within IF statements and interrupt service routines

  Accumulator (ACC):

    o Hold the data currently being processed by the CPU
    o Data is placed in the ACC before and after being processed in the ALU

  Memory Address Register (MAR):

    o Holds any addresses of memory from which data needs to be retrieved
    o This includes the address of the instruction **currently** being executed, before the instruction is fetched
    o Holds the address of the data on which the instruction is to be executed, before this data is fetched

  Memory Data Register (MDR):

    o Holds data/instructions after they have been fetched (from an address held in the MAR), including:
      ▪ Data to be used by the processor
      ▪ Data to be copied to an address
      ▪ The instruction before it is decoded
    o Acts as a buffer between main memory and the rest of the processor – all instructions and data enter/leave main memory and the CPU via being held in the MDR

Current Instruction Register (CIR):
- ○ Contains the instruction to be decoded (before it is executed), copied from the MDR
- ○ The CIR splits the instruction into two parts:
  - ▪ The **opcode** is the instruction/operation to be carried out (e.g. ADD)
  - ▪ The opcode is sent to the CU, which sends control signals to the relevant parts of the processor to synchronize the opcode's execution
  - ▪ The **operand** is either:
    - The main memory address of the data on which the instruction is to be executed (more likely)
    - The data itself if an **immediate operand** has been used (less likely)
  - ▪ If the operand is an address, it's copied to the MAR so the data can be later retrieved and placed in the MDR
  - ▪ If the operand is an immediate operand, the data is copied directly to the MDR

General-purpose registers:
- Used by programmers to temporarily store instructions and/or data that's used by running programs

Buses:

- The **Internal Bus** is the system of wires that allows binary communication between the different registers in the CPU
- There are 3 types of 'buses':
  - ○ The **data bus** carries data
  - ○ The **address bus** carries the address of the memory location to be accessed
  - ○ The **control bus** carries control signals about the status of various devices (e.g. whether the power supply is sufficient enough to allow the CPU to work), in this case whether data is read from or written to the said location

The Fetch, Decode, Execute Cycle:

This is the cycle conducted by the processor every time an instruction is executed

- The PC (Program Counter) contains the RAM address of the next instruction to be executed
- This instruction is copied to the MAR, from RAM via the data bus fetched and placed in the MDR
- The PC is incremented to point to the address of the next instruction in the queue
- The fetched instruction is copied from the MDR to the CIR
- The CIR splits the instruction into its **opcode** and **operand**
- The opcode is sent to the CU, which sends control signals to the rest of the processor to coordinate the instruction's execution
- The operand (address of data to be executed) is sent to the MAR; the data is fetched and placed in the MDR
  - ○ Alternatively, the operand is placed directly in the MAR if an **immediate operand** (the data itself) is used
- The data is sent to the accumulator, where it's held before being processed in the ALU

Fetch instruction from memory → Decode instruction → Execute instruction

> **Serial processing** – one instruction is processed at a time
> **Sequential processing** – one instruction is processed at a time <u>until completion</u>

Factors affecting performance of the CPU:

Clock speed:
- o The clock (in the CU) produces electrical impulses to coordinate parts of the CPU
- o Naturally, a faster clock speed means the processor can deal with a greater number of instructions/operations per second

Number of cores:
- o A multi-core processor is a single component consisting of multiple processing units called **cores** that fetch, decode and execute instructions individually at once
- o **SIMD** (Single Instruction, Multiple Data) processors have multiple cores that all perform the same instruction at once on different pieces of data – this is typically used in weather forecasting
  - **Vector/Array** processors have multiple ALUs that each simultaneously perform the same instruction on the different values in an array (for arrays, see page 37)
- o **Coprocessors** are specially-allocated cores that are optimized for a particular task (e.g. dealing with GPUs or floating-point operations) – this reduces the burden on any 'ordinary' processors

Cache:
- o **Level 1 cache** is usually part of the CPU itself and is the smallest (generally 8-64kb) and fastest (e.g. the registers on page 4)
- o **Level 2 cache** supplies variables currently being used by the processor, and is again very small (generally 256kb or 512kb) and fast
- o **Level 3 cache** holds the CPU's older variables and has a moderate size/speed

- o The more cache there is, the more data that can be stored **close to the CPU** (meaning it can be accessed faster)

Von Neumann computer architecture:

- Uses a single control unit
- Programs and data stored together in main memory in the same format
- Data and instructions share the same data bus; this can be problematic since data and instructions often need to be fetched at **different rates**, often slower than the rate at which the CPU can execute instructions – this is known as the **von Neumann bottleneck**
- Hence, the processor requires two clock cycles to complete an instruction:
  1. Fetch the instruction from memory and decode it
  2. Execute the instruction, including fetching required data
- Uses the fetch, decode, execute cycle as a machine cycle, thus only executing one instruction at a time – this is a **sequential (or serial) processing machine**
- **Programs can easily alter themselves** since they're stored in read-write memory (to enable the data to be changed); this includes writing their own executable outputs to memory – programs can, essentially, write themselves

Harvard computer architecture:

- The memory is split into two parts; one for data and another for instructions
- These two parts of memory are accessed with different buses (the data bus and program bus)
- This means the CPU can be accessing both data and instructions simultaneously
- Appropriate pipelining can allow an instruction to be completed in one clock cycle
- Program memory is typically read-only, whilst data memory is read-write (hence, a program cannot alter its own contents without replacing it completely)

Contemporary computer arcitecture:

- Modern computers combine elements from both the Von Neumann and Harvard architectures

Different devices have different uses and, hence, use different processor architectures according to their individual benefits.

Complex Instruction Set Computer (CISC) processors:

- More complex hardware
- More complex instruction set (e.g. ADDLOTS means LOAD, ADD, STORE)
- Requires multiple cycles per instruction since each is more complex
- Many addressing modes and instructions available
- Less work for compiler to translate code (since less instructions per process)
- Less RAM space required – code is more compact
- Closer to high level (spoken) language
- Unpredictable decode/execute times
- Larger load on CPU – CISC commands erase all registers automatically for each new instruction
- Uses more than one register set (ways in which the registers can be optimized)
- E.g. desktop or laptop computers

> **Words such as ADDLOTS or ADD that represent instructions are known as _mnemonics_**

Reduced Instruction Set Computer (RISC) processors:

- Simpler instructions (LOAD, ADD, STORE) but more of them per process
- Requires more RAM to store instructions – code is less compact
- More work for compiler (more instructions per process)
- Less addressing modes and instructions available
- Decode/execute times are more predictable – generally requires one cycle per instruction since all are equally simple
- Reduces CPU work by only altering necessary registers
- Uses more than one register set (ways in which the registers can be optimized)
- E.g. smartphones and tablets (pipelining is more important for smaller processors)

Types of processing/system:

Serial/sequential processing:

- One process is attended to at a time (serial)
- The process runs until completion (sequential)

Multicore processing:

- A single physical processor incorporates the logic of multiple processors within a single integrated unit
- This allows multiple tasks to be processed simultaneously
- Cores will likely share Level 2/3 cache but will have their own registers
- Generally used with **parallel processing** (e.g. MIMD processors)

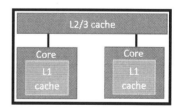

Parallel processing:

- Processes are split into parts and shared across multiple cores simultaneously (uses **multicore processing**)
- This allows them to be completed in the shortest possible time
- Software has to be optimized for parallel processing to make efficient use of it
- Parallel processing was developed as software became more complex and hence demanded more processing power for fast execution

A computer system will almost always need to communicate with other computer systems/ people and will require an effective way of storing data.

Hardware: the physical parts of a computer system
Software: instructions/programs that enable the hardware to work usefully, fulfilling an end-user's requirements

Examples of input devices:

- Keyboard (button press -> binary -> character set -> output)
    - Used for manual data entry
    - May be onscreen (using a touchscreen/mouse) or a separate device
- Mouse (sensor/button press -> change in x/y direction on screen/selections)
    - Used to select different options on a screen
- Webcam (light sensor -> data stream -> output)
    - Used to transmit live video for video chats
    - Used to monitor rooms (e.g. in factories)
- Touchscreen (electrostatic grid -> changes in current detected)
    - Used where a mouse/keyboard would be too large or vulnerable (e.g. smartphones, tourist information points)
    - Optimised for use with menu-based operating systems
- Barcode scanner (light/laser -> waveforms detected from reflection of light)
    - Used in shops to identify particular items
- Microphone (audio sensor -> data stream)
    - Used to transmit audio for use in calls or monitoring

> **You'll be expected to recognise the input/output requirements of different computer systems during the exam.**

Examples of output devices:

- Speakers (data stream -> amplified audio)
    - Used to provide audio information (e.g. at tourist information points)
    - Used to play music
- Monitor, Visual Display Unit (data stream -> imagine produced on monitor)
    - Displays the user interface of the device
    - Used to provide visual information (e.g. displaying programs on a laptop)
- Motor (interprets program outputs ->movements)
    - Used for specific, physical operations (e.g. in factories)
- Printer (data -> dot matrix/inkjet/laser)
    - Used to provide hard-copies of information (e.g. in offices)

Types of storage device:

- Magnetic:
    - ✓ High data transfer rate
    - ✓ Non-volatile
    - ✓ Large capacities
    - ✗ Not portable – contains moving parts that may break if moved
    - ✗ Can be noisy
    - E.g. Hard Disc Drives (HDDs):
        - Used as permanent storage for the computer's main files
- Flash:
    - ✓ Non-volatile
    - ✓ Contain no moving parts (solid-state – unlikely to break and hence portable); electrical impulses are used to imprint data
    - ✓ Used to transport data – light and robust
    - ✓ High transfer rate
    - ✓ All data takes the same amount of time to be accessed (data is read at the speed of light), meaning defragmentation is useless

- x   Degrades over time
- x   Expensive to produce and hence only available with small capacities
- o   E.g. SD cards, USB sticks, EEPROM (Electronically Erasable Programmable ROM)
- o   Optical:
  - ✓   Cheaper than most forms of storage
  - ✓   Non-volatile
  - ✓   Moderate capacity
  - ✓   Disks are light and portable
  - x   Slow data transfer rate – hence generally better suited to domestic uses rather than large-scale commercial ones
  - x   Disks can easily scratch
    - o   E.g. CD-ROM – data is written during the manufacturing process
    - o   E.g. CD-R/ DVD-R – data can be written by the user but only once
    - o   E.g. CD-RW/DVD-RW- data can be written and rewritten by the user
- o   Random Access Memory (RAM):
  - o   Stores data and instructions for programs currently running on the device (including the operating system itself)
  - o   Volatile (relies on an electrical current – RAM is cleared when the device turns off)
  - o   Fast, since running program data must be quickly accessed and changed for the program to run quickly
- o   Read-Only Memory (ROM):
  - o   Write-once, non-volatile memory
  - o   Stores data that you won't want to change (e.g. BIOS – see page 15 – it's required as soon as the device is turned on)

Virtual Storage (storage virtualisation):

- o   Multiple storage devices on a network are integrated and appear as a single device
- o   This allows a single storage drive to have a size that can vary depending on its requirements by adding/removing storage devices
- o   The individual devices are easier to manage and can be configured using the same settings

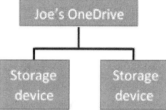

The operating system is a set of core programs that allows the computer system to run as a useful device by controlling/managing hardware, the user interface and other running software. As a result, the complexity of the hardware is hidden.

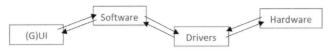

The purpose of operating systems:

1. **Controls hardware** (managing system resources) through software such as hardware drivers or system software. This includes allocating memory/processor time to individual devices (see scheduling – page 13).

2. **Provides a platform for applications to run** and deals with software issues such as the storage of application files, memory management, etc.

3. **Provides a user interface** for the operator, allowing communication between the hardware and the user by accepting and translating user commands, displaying messages, confirming successful inputs, displaying running programs, etc.

4. **Handles translation of code** using translators: a compiler/interpreter translates program code to assembly language, and an assembler (see page 18) translates the assembly code to machine code (binary that's executed by the CPU).

5. **Contains utility programs** to manage and maintain hardware (e.g. defragmentation, firewalls, antivirus, task management).

6. **Handles communications** using protocols (rules) to govern the communication (see page 29).

Primary memory management:

Types of memory:

1. Primary

   o RAM (volatile)
   o Temporarily stores instructions and data of running programs since they will need to be executed quickly
   o Smaller but faster

2. Secondary

   o Backing storage (non-volatile)
   o Stores permanent data
   o Larger but slower than primary

The purpose of memory management:

- All software runs and all data is stored on a form of memory – hence, it's very important
- All memory is finite (limited in size)
- The memory manager (a utility program) manages the use of primary memory to maximise its efficiency:
  - o Prevents programs/data (including the OS) from overriding each other in memory by allocating them separate areas that only they can see
  - o Converts logical addresses to physical ones
  - o Deals with memory allocation during paging/segmentation (see next pages)
  - o Reallocates memory when necessary
  - o Allows programs larger than main memory to run

Paging:

- Main memory is **partitioned** into physical divisions called 'pages'
- When a computer is running short of primary memory, it uses parts of secondary memory as primary memory (so programs don't have to be shut down completely) – this is known as **virtual memory**
- The memory manager tries to make primary and secondary memory appear continuous/seamless
- This allows more programs to be able to run simultaneously on a device

- This also allows programs that are larger than primary memory's capacity to run, since the idle parts of the program can be stored in virtual memory
- When primary memory is almost full, inactive pages are moved temporarily from primary to virtual memory
- When an application needs data held on a page in virtual memory, it will be swapped back into main memory and another inactive page may take its place
- To manage these pages, a 'page table' is created by the memory manager to store the starting address of each page (where the first byte of the page is located in physical memory)
- All pages are the **same size**
- Page sizes can range from 512 bytes to 64kb
- Pages do not need to be continuous (stored one after the other)

Segmentation (primary memory partitioning):

- Primary memory is partitioned into **logical divisions** that hold sections of program data
- These 'segments' of memory do **not** have fixed sizes

Stack segment:

- Starts from the top and grows downwards
- Holds variables and return addresses of subroutines (see page 39– call stack)

Free memory:

- Free space allows the stack to grow and shrink

Data segment:

- Where data used by the running code (e.g. variables) are stored

Code segment:

- Where the program code itself is stored

Paging VS segmentation:

- Similarities:
  - Both split primary memory into smaller sections
  - Both aim to maximise the use of primary memory
  - Neither require an entire program to be loaded into primary memory; more can be called upon when it's needed
  - Both use indexing to access rarely-used code
  - Both are placed in non-continuous memory addresses
- Differences:

  > An exam question may ask you to compare the two...

  - Pages are smaller than segments (in size)
  - **Only segments** vary in size
  - Non-continuous pages do not affect performance (since a page table is used) but segments prefer to be in one piece to limit the searching required by the memory manager

  *Segmentation: **logical** memory divisions (e.g. storing all instructions together)*
  Pages: physical memory divisions (each page is a separate area of memory)

Virtual memory:

- Primary memory is finite
- The memory manager uses virtual memory to 'fool' running programs into thinking there is more primary memory available
- The running program uses virtual addresses rather than real (physical) ones when instructing where data/instructions should be stored – the operating system is tasked with allocating a real memory address to every virtual one that the program uses (each virtual address is **mapped** to a physical one) using a memory management unit (MMU)
- This means that a running program does not deal with the primary memory (RAM) addresses directly and so the system is more secure since programs have no way of altering the other programs stored in memory

Problems with memory management:

- Disk thrashing:
  - Swapping pages in and out of main memory can take longer than the actual processing of the pages – this means little useful processing is done

- Memory leaks:
  - A program will reserve itself main memory; badly written programs will not give up this space when it's no longer needed
  - Hence, large amounts of memory become 'locked up', meaning they cannot be used; the main memory is largely empty but is considered full

- Memory crashes:
  - Badly written programs may try to write data outside of the memory allocated to them
  - Nowadays, memory managers will prevent this and the program will likely crash
  - Previously, this conflicted code could have caused a bluescreen error

- Stack overflow:
  - Poorly written programs may cause functions to continuously need to access new functions
  - This may cause the call stack (see page 39) to overflow, having either met its maximum size or having overflowed into the data segment below
    E.g.:

```
FOR (int i = 1; i > 0, i++){

    do something;

}
```

This is an example of a <u>recursion error</u>

Interrupts:

- Interrupts are signals (from either attached devices or programs running within the OS) that cause the CPU to pause, consider the signal and act accordingly
- Most modern computers are interrupt-driven – they execute whatever is next in the queue instead of waiting for (slower) I/O devices to respond (which would waste time)
- An interrupt may instruct a new program to run
- An interrupt handler (part of the scheduler, see next page) prioritises interrupts and saves them in a queue, should multiple occur at once
- **Interrupt service routines** (ISRs) are software routines that invoke responses to an interrupt – the interrupt will instruct this ISR to run

---

Hardware interrupts: devices indicate that they require attention (e.g. keyboard presses)
Software interrupts: typically caused when a program detects an error or illegal operation

---

Interrupts within the Fetch, Decode, Execute Cycle (see page 5):

- An interrupt can occur at any point during the execution of an instruction
- When this occurs, the following steps are taken to ensure that the cycle can be resumed once the interrupt has been dealt with:
  - Suspend the execution of the current instruction and move it back into the queue
  - Save the contents of registers in a stack so that they can be retrieved once the interrupt has been dealt with
  - Load the program counter with the address of the interrupt service routine and continue the cycle with a greater priority
  - Once the execution of the interrupt service routine is complete, the address of the next instruction in the queue (probably the one that was paused) is fetched and the cycle continues as normal

Scheduling:

- **Scheduling**: the way in which a **multitasking** OS orders tasks for the CPU (in terms of priority)
- **Processes**: parts of programs loaded into memory that are potentially executed by the CPU

The purpose of scheduling:

- Process as many jobs as possible (in a certain time)
- Hence, make maximum use of CPU time
- Makes programs appear responsive to the user (so delays are not noticed)
- Maximise the use of resources such as I/O devices
- Give fair CPU allocation to all current processes – leave none waiting for too long
- Alter priorities of processes based on the scheduler algorithms used (see next page)
- Avoid 'deadlock', where nothing is processed because all processes are waiting for others
- The ideal scheduler would make 100% use of the CPU

A process can be in one of three states:

1. Blocked:
   - Not running/not able to run
   - Waiting for a resource (e.g. interrupt, available memory, etc.)
2. Ready:
   - Ready to run but not currently active in the CPU (queued)
   - Will run when the CPU is free (and the process has the highest priority)
3. Running:
   - Code currently being processed in the CPU

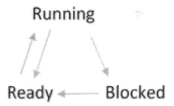

Scheduler algorithms:

1. **First Come, First Served**
   o The scheduler prioritises processes by the order in which they arrive
   o Hence, the first to arrive is first to run in the CPU
   o

2. **Shortest Burst / Shortest Job First**
   o Processes with the shortest burst times are executed first
   o This improves user response times (since user inputs are simple and thus prioritised), making the UI appear more responsive

> **Burst time:** the time a process would take to execute in one go

3. **Shortest Time Remaining**
   o Like a mixture between Round Robin and Shortest Burst
   o All processes are allocated an equal run time, but the processes requiring less overall CPU time are prioritised

4. **Multi-Level feedback**
   o There are multiple queues with different priorities over one another
   o The queues may be organised (e.g. I/O processes, program processes, etc.)
   o This may be combined with other forms of prioritisation within each individual queue

Types of operating system:

1. **Distributed**
   o A type of network OS
   o Nodes (devices) are connected to the network and processing is shared between them
   o This maintains efficiency of processor-use across all nodes
   o **No shared memory**, since it would be inefficient to search the memory of all nodes on the network to locate something
   o *E.g. Google's server warehouses*

2. **Embedded**
   o Built for one specific task
   o Does not have the hardware or instruction set to do anything beyond what is intended (this would be wasted)
   o *E.g. the OS in an individual traffic light*

3. **Multi-tasking**
   o Contains a processor that can process billions of instructions per second
   o Hence, multiple programs can run at once; it seems as if they are being processed simultaneously
   o **Time slicing** is used: each process is allocated a certain (very small) amount of processing time before moving on to the next
   o Running programs are separated into individual windows
   o *E.g. playing music whilst typing an essay*

4. **Multi-user**

   - A form of multi-tasking OS that has several connected terminals
   - NOTE: the terminals are **not individual devices**: they all rely on the same operating system and hardware to function (<u>one device, may users</u>)
   - Time slicing is used to give each terminal a fair (and very small) amount of processing time, **in turn**, so they appear responsive
   - Priorities may be used to dictate the order of processing
   - Data from each terminal is separated in memory to maintain data security
   - *E.g. a tourist information system in a large city*

5. **Real time**

   - Data is processed immediately after it is received
   - Hence, outputs are constantly produced based on the inputs received
   - Used in systems where responses to inputs **must occur immediately**
   - *E.g. computer games consoles, air bag systems*

Basic Input / Output System (BIOS):

- The program a computer system's microprocessor uses to boot after it's turned on
- The program that manages data flow between the OS and other connected devices (hard disk, video adapter, keyboard, mouse, printer, etc.)
- Controls CPU frequencies and RAM timings
- May provide alternate boot/hardware management options for users (e.g. altering fan speed), but only has around 1MB of main memory
- Software stored in ROM since it will never need to change and should not be changed to maintain data security
- Specific to the motherboard
- Contains details of attached hardware
- Runs the Power-On Self-Test (POST):
  - The diagnostic testing sequence run by the BIOS when the device is powered on
  - POST checks that all the appropriate hardware (keyboard, RAM, disk drives, etc. in a Personal Computer) is present and functions as intended

Device drivers:

- Instructions used by the OS to operate with a peripheral
- Includes communication protocols (see page 29)
- Provides settings to configure hardware for use with the OS
- Hundreds come preinstalled on the operating system and specific ones can be downloaded
- The drivers for a specific device are stored within a file known as a registry or directory
- The drivers convert general inputs/outputs from the operating system into code that will run on the intended device (and vice-versa)

Virtual machines:

- A theoretical computer that provides an environment with its own translator
- This is an OS installed on software that imitates the dedicated hardware of a different device, e.g. running macOS on a Windows device
- Uses **intermediate code:**
  - Simplified code between high-level and machine language
  - Produced by a compiler and run by an interpreter
  - Can be interpreted by any device with the relevant virtual machine installed
  - Allows code portability between devices of different architectures/languages
  - This means different parts of a program can be written in different languages by different programmers suited to their purposes and then compiled to the same intermediate language
  - Different virtual machines have different interpreters to translate intermediate code to machine code for execution with the device's particular hardware
  - Syntax error free – any such errors would have been detected when first translated

Software is used for a plethora of reasons and exists in many different forms.

- **Software:** instructions and data that enable hardware to produce useful results and fulfil a user's requirements
- **Applications software:** solves problems and performs user-defined tasks (produces useful results for the user)
- **System software:** the set of programs needed to control/manage the hardware of the system, allowing applications software to run

Generic software:

- General purpose; can do a range of tasks
- Replicates real-life tasks (spreadsheets, databases, email, presentation, word processing, graphics)
- Available for immediate use – can be bought and installed straight away (e.g. via downloads)
- Having multiple uses may make the software complicated
- Cheaper since more popular
- Evaluation (trial) period often available before buying
- Large number of users – software will be well documented and training may be available
- Tried and tested before (and after) release – fewer bugs likely

Bespoke software (see SDLC – page 70):

- Written for a specific, uncommon task for a specific group of people (e.g. for use on a factory floor)
- Has specific program content/a specific UI based on a specific user's requirements
- Takes a long time to produce
- Expensive since it involves a long collaboration between the developers and end users
- Runs on user-specified hardware
- May be integrated with other, specific software
- Dedicated training/support available (from whoever made the software)
- Upgrades will exactly match the users' requirements, should they change

> NOTE: do not refer to specific examples of software in the exam unless asked – refer to them under their general names (e.g. presentation software, not PowerPoint)

Integrated packages (e.g. Microsoft Office):

- Similar, familiar UI across all programs
- Cheaper and easier than buying the individual programs of the package separately
- Often cater for a wide range of related purposes/needs
- Inter-compatible – files created in one program may be compatible with all/other programs in the package (e.g. a spreadsheet within a word document)

Utility software:

- Systems software (part of the operating system) designed to manage hardware and/or run software:
    o File sorting, naming, conversion and repair
    o Disk defragmentation, partitioning and monitoring
    o Printing
    o Backups of files
    o Antivirus
    o Firewalls

Open source software:

- Source code is available to the general public for use/modification from original design
- Intended to be a collaborative effort – programmers improve the released source code and share their changes within the community
- Often free
- Updates from the developers can be random, if at all
- May lack the features of rival, closed source software
- May have less dedicated support from the developers
- May include advertisements to produce revenue for the developers

Propriety (closed source) software:

- The software is owned by an individual/company
- There are almost always major restrictions on its use
- The source code is almost always kept hidden and is unchangeable
- Software may be larger and harder to learn
- More updates will generally be provided by the developers
- Often greater levels of testing and, hence, less bugs in the programs

Forms of code:

- 1st Generation: machine code directly executed by the CPU (binary)

- 2nd Generation: assembly languages (simple words/instructions, e.g. LMC's instruction set – see page 22)

- 3rd Generation: 'imperative' source code (meaning it's written by a programmer and contains step-by-step instructions on how to solve a problem) which is converted to machine code when executed

- 4th Generation: 'declarative' (meaning it declares what is required rather than how to achieve what is required) and similar to natural language, used by people with little or no programming skill/knowledge (e.g. database manipulation, mail merges)

Translators: programs that transfer written code from one language to another without <u>changing the original meaning of the code</u>

Three types of translator:

**Comparison questions
are likely!**

Compiler:
- Translates high-level code to assembly language
- <u>All</u> of the high level code is checked, translated and executed <u>at once</u>
- Hence, the translated code can be taken and used as an executable in one go
- Bad for programming development (there cannot be any errors before the program can run since each line is required)
- Uses more memory, since all of the running code is loaded into RAM at once
- Faster, since all of the code is processed in one go

Interpreter:

- Also translates high-level code to assembly language
- Checks, translates then executes high level code, <u>one line at a time</u>
- Once the line has been processed, it is discarded from RAM and replaced with the next
- Errors are reported as they are encountered
- Good for program development, since the code will execute until an error is found (and identify the line of the error) and can begin running from any line/one line at a time using **single stepping/break points**
- Uses less memory, since only one line is processed (and hence stored in RAM) at a time
- Slower, since one line is processed at a time and then removed

Assembler:
- Converts assembly language to machine code (binary that is directly executed by the CPU)
- Mnemonic opcodes (e.g. ADD) are replaced with machine code
- Symbolic addresses are replaced with numeric addresses
- Checks syntax and offers diagnostics for errors found
- Reserves main memory for instructions/data
- Creates a symbol table to match labels to addresses for retrieving instructions/data

> Since different machines have different CPU instruction sets, each programming language
> needs a different translator for each type of machine

You'll need to be familiar with several different aspects of programming that are commonly used or considered during program development.

Program flow:

- Programs will always execute from top to bottom
- In a single line of code, the <u>order of operations</u> is always followed:
    1. Parenthetical statements (those inside of parenthesis) are computed first
    2. Everything to the right of an assignment statement (if there is one) is computed
    3. The assignment itself (if there is one) is computed
- **Control statements** affect the line of code that is next to be executed:
    o Branches (such as IF statements) are lines of code that cause the computer to deviate from its default sequence of execution
    o Loops may cause code to be repeatedly executed either a set number of times or based on a condition
    o Function calls may tell the computer to execute code from a different function
    o Statements such as 'break' or 'continue' can be used to pause/resume the execution of a program at a certain point

Variables vs constants:

- Both:
    o An identifier/name
    o Associated with a particular memory location that may hold a value
    o Identifiers cannot be reserved words (e.g. 'if') or have spaces
    o Identifiers are case-sensitive
- Variables:
    o Use CamelCasing as a naming convention
    o Does not need to be declared with a value
    o Used to store/manipulate data which can change while the program is running
- Constants:
    o Uses ALL_CAPITALS as a naming convention
    o Cannot change its value while the program is running
    o Value must be declared when the constant is declared

Functions vs procedures:

Functions:

- A named (has an identifier) section of a program that performs a specific task
- Returns a single value
- Generally takes parameters
- Used as part of an expression; often called an inline
    o e.g. `int x = sqrt(4);`
    o sqrt is the function being called in this case – the value '4' is the parameter

Procedures:

- Also a named sub-section of code that performs a specific task
- Does not usually take parameters or return a value
- Used as an instruction/statement
- E.g. `clearHistory();`

Operators - characters that represent actions:

Assignment operator:

=   Assigns a value on its right to the identifier on its left

Arithmetic operators within Java:

+   Addition (and String concatenation)
-        Subtraction
*   Multiplication
/   Division
%   Mod (Remainder)
^   Exponential   Math.pow(a, b) = a^b (in Java)

Boolean operators within Java (see 1.4.3 for more info):

|| OR
&&   AND
^   XOR
!   NOT

Comparative/Relational operators:

==	EQUAL TO	<	LESS THAN
!=	NOT EQUAL TO	>	GREATER THAN
<=	LESS THAN OR EQUAL TO	>=	GREATER THAN OR EQUAL TO

String handling in Java:

- Strings are a group of characters ('chars') that can be manipulated:
- `String newString = "Hello, world!";`
  declares a new string with the identifier **newString**, containing "Hello, world!"
- `newString.toUpperCase()`
  would return "HELLO, WORLD!"
- `newString.toLowerCase()`
  would return "hello, world!"
- `newString.length()`
  would return the length of the string (the number of chars, including spaces): 13
- Strings in Java use **zero-based indexing**, meaning that the first character in the string is considered to be at position zero
- `newString.substring(0, 3)`
  would return the characters in positions 0 to, but not including, 3: "Hel"
- `newString.substring(3)`
  would return every character from position 3 onwards until the end of the string – "lo, world!"
- `newString.substring(newString.length()-3)`
  would return the last 3 characters of the string (the characters from the third-to-last position onwards: "ld!"
- `String secondString = newString.substring(0,4) + "cheese";`
  Creates a new string called secondString, made from the first four characters of newString and the word "cheese": "Hellcheese". Joining strings is called **concatenation**
- `newString.indexOf("el")`
  would return the first index in which "el" appears: 1
- `newString.endsWith("re")`
  would return whether the string ends in "re": FALSE
- `newString.charAt(3)`
  would return the char (character) at index 3

File handling:

• You may be asked to estimate the size of a file...

Units of storage:

- • 1 **bit**
- • 8 bits = 1 **byte**
- • 1024 bytes = 1 **kilobyte**
- • 1024 kilobytes = 1 **megabyte**
- • 1024 megabytes = 1 **gigabyte**, etc....

Some datatypes and their sizes:

- • **Integer**: 2 bytes
- • **Real (floating point)**: 4 bytes
- • **Date**: 8 bytes
- • **Boolean**: 1 byte
- • **String/Char**: 1 byte per character

- Fields/Attributes:

  o A collection of pieces of data of a certain datatype
  o Describes a particular characteristic of the records (like a category)
  o Has an identifier (e.g. Product Code)

- Records:

  o A collection of fields that give information about a particular entity
  o Has a unique identifier called a **primary key** (see Databases – page 23)

Fields

File

Records

Product Code	Description	Quantity	Date of Last Delivery	Perishable
...	...	...	...	...
QB578	Socks	100	01/02/2012	False
AX678	Cream Cakes	42	07/02/2012	True
PQ301	Pens	70	11/12/2011	False
DS871	Toasters	22	06/10/2011	False
KL651	Bananas	60	04/02/2012	True
...	...	...	...	...

Changing files in exam pseudocode:

- • `myFile = openRead("example.txt")` opens the file "example.txt" under the identifier "myFile"
  `x = myFile.readLine()` creates a variable "x" equal to the current line - allowing you to write to it
- • `myFile.writeLine("Hello, world!")` writes "Hello, world!" to the current line
- • `myFile.endOfFile()` identifies the end of the file
  `myFile.close()` closes the file

Assembly language:

- Assembly language is the programming language that is compiled within the CPU
- This consists of much more basic instructions compared to programming languages such as Java
- Although basic, the CPU will process often billions of these instructions per second
- These instructions consist of an **opcode** (the operation code to be carried out, such as ADD) and an **operand** (the address (e.g. in RAM) of the data on which the instruction is to be carried out)
- Opcodes like ADD are **mnemonics**; each has a unique instruction in memory associated with it
- DAT is an example of symbolic addressing – instead of referring to a specific memory location for an element, the assembler will resolve it to one automatically

The Little Man Computer:

- A program written to model a simple Von Neumann computer

Instruction	Mnemonic	Description
Load	LDA	Load the contents of the given mailbox onto the accumulator
Store	STA	Store the contents of the accumulator to the mailbox of the given address
Add	ADD	Add the contents of the given mailbox onto the accumulator
Subtract	SUB	Subtract the contents of the given mailbox from the accumulator
Input	INP	Copy the value from the "in box" onto the accumulator
Output	OUT	Copy the value from the accumulator to the "out box".
End	HLT	Causes the Little Man Computer to stop executing your program.
Branch if Zero	BRZ	If the contents of the accumulator are 000, the PC (program counter) will be set to the given address
Branch if Zero or positive	BRP	If the contents of the accumulator are 000 or positive (i.e. the negative flag is not set), the PC (program counter) will be set to the given address
Branch always	BRA	Set the contents of the accumulator to the given address
Data storage	DAT	When compiled, a program converts each instruction into a three-digit code. These codes are placed in sequential mailboxes. Instead of a program component, this instruction will reserve the next mailbox for data storage

- You need to know how to <u>write</u> and understand basic LMC programs, such as the one below:

INP	Takes an input
STA FIRST	Stores the input under identifier 'FIRST'
INP	Takes an input
STA SECOND	Stores the input under identifier 'SECOND'
SUB FIRST	Subtracts the value of 'FIRST' from the value in the accumulator ('SECOND')
BRP SECONDBIG	If the accumulator holds a positive value, the code branches to 'SECONDBIG'
LDA FIRST	The value in the accumulator is replaced with the value of 'FIRST'
OUT	Outputs the value in the accumulator
BRA ENDPROGRAM	Branches (always) to 'ENDPROGRAM'
SECONDBIG LDA SECOND	Declares the code segment 'SECONDBIG' which first loads 'SECOND' into accumulator
OUT	Outputs the value in the accumulator
ENDPROGRAM HLT	Declares the code segment 'END PROGRAM' which stops execution
FIRST DAT	Declares the variable FIRST as a piece of data (replacing DAT with 001 would give it the value 1
SECOND DAT	Declares the variable SECOND as a piece of data

- The code above stores two inputs and outputs the largest

- If SECOND – FIRST is positive (meaning SECOND is the larger of the two), the code branches to SECONDBIG where SECOND is loaded and outputted before reaching HLT which stops execution

- If SECOND – FIRST isn't positive (meaning they're equal or FIRST is the larger of the two), FIRST is loaded and outputted, then the code branches to ENDPROGRAM where the execution is stopped

- You can try using LMC for yourself at http://peterhigginson.co.uk/LMC/

Databases are used to hold large amounts of data, often for use by applications.

- A **persistent**, **organised collection** of **related data**
  - o Persistent: stored in non-volatile, permanent memory (maintained when data handling applications (e.g. Excel) are no longer running)
  - o Organised collection: data is structured using tables, records and fields to make it easier for users/applications to add, delete, edit, search and manipulate data
  - o Related: individual records have a connection (e.g. customers of a company)

Entities	**Attribute/Field**
- The 'type' of record stored (e.g. customer)	- Each entity has attributes/fields
- A group of people/objects/events on which data can be held	- These are the properties of entities (e.g. for patients: DOB, address, allergies, etc.)
- Entities in a hospital database would be patient, nurse, ward, etc.	- Each has a single datatype

Flat-file databases:

- A simple database that stores all data in a single table (e.g. a single text file or spreadsheet)
- Advantages:
  - ✓ Useful for **simple, small lists** (e.g. an address book)
  - ✓ Algorithms required to manipulate the data are simpler
  - ✓ Requires only **basic hardware**/storage to manage and maintain the data (cheaper)
- Disadvantages:
  - x **Data redundancy**: storage is wasted when data is unnecessarily duplicated (e.g. multiple appointments for the same customer; customer's data is repeated for each appointment)
  - x Makes data entry **slower** since all data is entered manually and often multiple times
  - x **Reduced data integrity**: repeatedly inputting the same data increases the likelihood of errors (inaccurate data) through inconsistent data entry; there is no ability to implement error-checking
  - x **Difficult and slow to update** when all records need to be changed in a certain way
  - x **Data security**: all users have access to the same (all of the) data; there is no ability to implement access rights to the data beyond password-protecting the file itself - if you wanted to limit how much of the data was seen by someone, you'd need to create a new copy of the file with only the relevant data – this causes further issues if the data needs to be updated or is regularly changing
  - x Program-Data dependence: the user-interface of the program used is tied to the file such that the file cannot be changed without using the program
  - x Often only one person can access or change the data at any time

Relational databases:

- Many databases or tables, interrelated using primary and foreign keys (see page 26) as relationships, accessed using a DBMS (Database Management System)
- Advantages:
  - ✓ **Data redundancy is reduced**:
    - o Keys are used to link to data from other tables, meaning it only needs to be entered/stored once
    - o This is more efficient: it saves time and human resources
    - o It also means less storage is required
  - ✓ **Data integrity**:
    - o Constraints on the data can ensure it is in the correct format, range, etc. (like error-checking)
    - o New, custom-written applications that use the database can be added without affecting the stored data
    - o This ensures data consistency for all users – all users see the same data
    - o Multiple users can access the data simultaneously and changes to data are seen immediately

- ✓ **Data security:**
    - ○ Passwords can be used to restrict access to certain tables
    - ○ DBMS can control permissions (e.g. read-only tables)
    - ○ Data validation and verification techniques can be used
    - ○ Different programs cannot overwrite data since it is stored separately
- ✓ **Flexibility:**
    - ○ Data drawn from different files/programs can be combined in different ways, allowing for collecting better-quality information
- - Disadvantages:
    - x Complicated to setup and maintain – requires dedicated expertise (i.e. paid professional(s))
    - x The software and hardware required is powerful and thus expensive
    - x All applications that access the data are affected if the database/hardware fails

Keys in databases:
- - Primary key:
    - ○ An attribute that uniquely identifies each record in a table, e.g. for instances where there are more than one 'John Smith'
    - ○ E.g. membership numbers, catalogue numbers, etc.
    - ○ Many databases can create one automatically if needed
- - Foreign key:
    - ○ The primary key of a record from another table
    - ○ Used to establish a relationship between the main table and other tables
    - ○ Reduces data redundancy
    - ○ E.g. a Customer Orders table may use a foreign key to reference the customer who made each order – this is the primary key of the customer from the Customers table

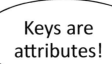

Keys are attributes!

- - Secondary key:
    - ○ An attribute that allows the records in a table to be sorted usefully (e.g. dates of birth)
    - ○ This allows for more efficient searching and data manipulation
    - ○ Different from the primary key
    - ○ Does not need to be unique
- - Composite/Compound key:
    - ○ A combination of two or more attributes in a table are used to uniquely identify each record (e.g. no two records in the Order Content table will have the same Order ID and Product ID)
- - Junction table:
    - ○ A table that references at least two other attributes, hence linking them (e.g. an Order Content table links Order IDs and Product IDs)
    - ○ Uses composite keys

Relationships and entity relationship diagrams:

- ERDs are used to describe the relationship between entities in a database

The three types of relationship:
- o One-to-one:
  - ▪ Quite rare
  - ▪ E.g. a student can only enrol on one course, and each course can only have one student enrolled (obviously, this is very unlikely in real life)
  - ▪ May be used for security reasons, e.g. separating payment details and customer details into two tables

- o Many-to-one:
  - ▪ E.g. a university student can only enrol on one course, but each course can have multiple students enrolled

- o Many-to-many:
  - ▪ E.g. a high school student can enrol on multiple courses, and each course can have multiple student enrolled

Database Management Systems (DBMSs):

- Software that handles the complexities of managing a database (listed below)
- May provide a user interface to allow interaction between the database managers and the data stored
- May use SQL (Standard Query Language) to communicate with other applications and manipulate the data
- May provide different views of the data for different users
- Tasks of a DBMS:
  - o Find data
  - o Add new data
  - o Update data
  - o Maintain indexes to aid indexed sequential file access
  - o Manage access rights
  - o Enforce data integrity rules/error checking
  - o Ensure data is stored securely on the storage medium (e.g. through encryption)
- Advantages:
  - ✓ All applications access the same data through the DBMS, meaning results are consistent for all
  - ✓ Allows use of access procedures to improve **data security** – only permitted individuals/applications can access certain data
  - ✓ Allows multiple applications to be able to access and change data simultaneously; updates changes to data immediately so all applications can see them
- Disadvantages:
  - ✗ Again expensive to set up and maintain due to the software, hardware and expertise required
  - ✗ Security of data is essential since large amounts of data are controlled centrally and hence are very vulnerable
  - ✗ It can be difficult to learn how to use a DBMS

Data dictionaries:

- A file containing descriptions of all the data in a database, stored in tables/as a relational database
- Used by database managers when altering the database structure
- Uses **metadata** (data that gives information about other data)
- E.g.
    o Names of tables/columns
    o Characteristics of data (type, length)
    o Restrictions on values
    o Relationships between data
    o Which programs can access data
    o Identifies primary/foreign keys

Standard database notation:

- Tables in databases are declared as follows:
    o **CUSTOMERS**(CustomerID, FirstName, LastName, etc...)
    o **ORDERS**(OrderID, OrderDate, CustomerID, etc...)
    o **ORDERCONTENT**(OrderID, ProductID, etc...)
- **Bold**/CAPS declares the table name
- Underlined declares the primary key
- Italics declares a foreign key
- Underlined and italics declares part of a composite key

Some methods of capturing data:

1. Voice recognition
    - E.g. phone-integrated AI such as Siri, Google Now
2. Optical Mark Recognition (OMR)
    - E.g. lottery tickets, some exams
3. Optical Character Recognition (OCR)
    - E.g. scanning word documents and converting them to a text format
4. Magnetic Ink Character Recognition (MICR)
    - E.g. cheques
5. Data Capture Forms
    - E.g. intelligent character recognition forms (set amounts of space)
6. Barcodes and QR codes
    - E.g. in shops, on promotional posters

Managing data and **database schemas**:

- These are examples of abstractions (see page 49) that are used to simplify the database's structure so it can be easily used - they help to manage the data in a database
- External view:
  - o As seen by the user
  - o A view designed to be useful for a particular job
  - o Generally a user-friendly interface
  - o Allows end-user to interact with the data in the database (indirectly, through an application)
  - o User does not need to be aware of the physical structure of the database or the data stored within it

- Conceptual view:
  - o Seen by database managers
  - o Concerns how the data is organised; a single view of all the data in the database that can be used to make changes
  - o Includes the design of tables, types of stored data, data validation rules, links between tables, data dictionaries etc.
  - o Requires knowledge of the database structure
  - o E.g. 'Design view' in MySQL Workbench (a DBMS)

- Physical/Internal view:
  - o Concerns how the data is stored on the storage medium
  - o Designers and users of the database are not concerned with this detail
  - o This is controlled/hidden by the DBMS
  - o Factors such as file-access methods used by the DBMS and connected applications (Indexed sequential, Random access, etc.) determine how the data is stored

Networks are a medium over which any number or type of device can share data.

Networks:

- "A number of devices ('nodes'), linked together in order to share resources: hardware (e.g. printers), software and data"
- Most large networks have at least one server: a powerful computer to manage the network, including perhaps providing services such as file storage or email

MAC address:

- A unique identifier to the network interface card on a device
- Consists of 6 pairs of hexadecimal values
- Hence 2^{48} possible combinations; MAC addresses will not run out in a long time

IP address:

- Identifies a device on a network
- Internal IP addresses identify a device on a local (e.g. home) network
- External IP addresses identify a router connected to the internet
- Changed from IPv4 to IPV6 when old IP addresses ran out

Benefits of networking:

- Sharing devices and resources (e.g. printers, internet access) saves equipment and thus money
- File sharing between users/devices allows for easier collaborative working
- Allows sharing and work over much larger geographical regions
- Users on a network can communicate via email or Instant Messenger
- One 'volume license' can be bought for all devices on a network, saving money compared to having to buy licences for each individual device
- Centralised management: all nodes can be managed from one central location (e.g. to install software on all at once)
- Joint security for all users (including firewalls and Internet restrictions to prevent accidental viruses entering the network)
- Restrictions (viewable folders, Internet access, runnable programs, etc.) to maintain user and system safety
- File storage; access files/accounts from different devices connected to the network

Limitations of networking:

- Difficult to implement and manage
- Expensive to implement and manage
- If a file server breaks, none of the stored files are accessible; large numbers of files belonging to many people could be lost
- Specific expertise is required, hence costing money
- Viruses can spread quickly between devices on a network
- Hacking is possible, and hence security features are required to prevent this – a large quantity of files must be protected
- Cables can be difficult and tedious to replace if broken, and breaks may affect large numbers of devices at once (see below)

Protocols:

- A set of rules necessary to govern communications between devices on a network
- *Protocols are needed because...*
    - o Different manufacturers create different systems with different architectures
    - o These architectures cannot communicate unless they agree on the same set of communication 'rules'
    - o Hence, protocols are these 'rules'

- *Protocol layering...*
    - o Collections of protocols are simplified by being split into functional sections
    - o Each layer has individual protocols assigned to them that deal with a particular aspect of the communication

- *The benefits of protocol layering...*
    - o Manufacturers can design systems to be compatible with particular layers
    - o Layers are ordered chronologically (in the order they would be followed) to simplify the creation of the protocol
    - o Changes to the protocol can be made by altering a single layer and the links to the other layers in contact with it

- *Good protocols handle...*
    - o How to set up/stop a connection
    - o How to start and end the data sent (headers and footers)
    - o How to deal with corrupted or missing data
    - o How to format and error-check data

- *Examples of **physical** protocols...*
    - o Wired/wireless
    - o Frequencies
    - o Serial/Parallel transmission
    - o Radio/Microwave
    - o Copper/Fibre-optic cabling

- *Examples of **logical** protocols...*
    - o Baud rate
    - o Error correction/checking techniques
    - o Packet size
    - o Compression techniques
    - o Encryption algorithms
    - o Digital signatures
    - o Routing
    - o Flow control

Don't look so excited…

<u>The network structure of the Internet:</u>

The TCP/IP (Transmission Control Protocol/Internet Protocol) Stack:
- Used for **packet switching** communications
- An example of an **abstraction** (see page 49) that's used to simplify the stack into understandable layers
- A collection of protocols used to govern communications between devices over the Internet
- Has 4 layers:
  - 1. Application
    - Ensures the data is formatted in a way appropriate to the type of application/data being sent, so that it can be understood by the recipient
    - Ensures the correct application protocols are used (e.g. http)
    - Thus allows the end user to interact with the application once it's received
    - DNS (Domain Name System) resolves the email/website address to an IP address if required
  - 2. Transport
    - When sending:
      - A virtual connection between the two communicating devices is established using a handshake signal
      - The appropriate port numbers (used to identify the protocols required and hence the types of application) are added
      - Defines the level of service and the connection status
    - When receiving:
      - Packets are reassembled in the right order
      - High-level error checking takes place
      - Packets with errors/Missing packets are re-requested (TCP only)
  - 3. Network/Internet
    - When sending:
      - The data is broken down into packets, which are numbered based on their order
      - Adds the IP address to port numbers, creating a **socket address** – one for the sender's information, another for the recipient's
      - This is added to each packet's source and destination addresses
      - This ensures the recipient knows where to send a confirmation
      - The packets are now **datagrams**
    - When receiving:
      - The IP address is removed from the packets
  - 4. Link/Network interface:
    - When sending:
      - Adds MAC addresses, identifying the sender's and recipient's unique network interface cards, to packets in a **frame header and footer**
      - Packets are moved over the communication medium via connected routers
    - When receiving:
      - Headers/footers removed from packets
      - Low-level error checking takes place

        <u>Sending:</u> Application -> Transport -> Network/Internet -> Link/Network interface
        <u>Receiving:</u> Link/Network interface -> Network/Internet -> Transport -> Application

DNS (Doman Name System) – a data exchange protocol:
- Used to resolve domain names (e.g. www.google.com) to IP addresses (e.g. 139.130.4.5)
- DNS servers exist around the world and contain databases of pairs of domain names and IP addresses, over which that individual server has authority
- These servers are managed by IT teams and behave as a single, integrated database
- Some web servers use static IP addresses (the IP address will not change if the network is disconnected), by resolving the IP address to the unique MAC address of the network interface card
- Domain names contain a hierarchy:
    1. Top level   www.moodle.suffolkone.ac.uk
    2. Second level   5   4   3   2 1
    3. Domain name   www.bbc.co.uk
    4. Subdomain name   5   3   2   1
    5. Host name
- There are 13 'Root Servers' around the world which act as a directory for all top-level domain names (.com, .info, .org, .uk, etc.)

Data sent via the internet uses protocol layering (see page 29)

Local Area Networks (LANs):
- Cover a small geographical area (school/office)
- High speed (1000mbps)
- Uses Ethernet or a Token Ring to connect nodes
- Data more secure

Wide Area Networks (WANs):
- Covers a large geographical area (more than one site) by connecting networks together
- Low speed (150mbps)
- Uses hardware optimized for long-distance communications (ATM, MPLS, Frame Relay)
- Data less secure; it's subject to interception

Circuit vs packet switching methodologies:
- Circuit switching:
    o A dedicated circuit connection is established between the two nodes
    o This connection is reserved (it cannot be used by anyone else) and remains open until the communication is complete
    o Packets flowing between the nodes will always follow this circuit; hence all packets are sent and received chronologically
    o The recipient sends a response every time a packet is received
    o If the circuit is broken, the connection is lost completely unless it can be rerouted
    o Used for time-critical transmissions (where data must arrive immediately)
- Packet switching:
    o All packets are sent individually and hence may take any route to the destination, including via other routers that redirect them
    o Since packets may not arrive chronologically, they're labelled with their order so they can be reassembled when received
    o Packets that do not arrive in time will be re-requested (only with TCP protocols)

	Advantages	Disadvantages
Circuit switching	- Allows realtime transmissions with little prospect of lag - No risk of data collisions as line is reserved - Packets' order does not have to be included since all are sent in order and along the same path; less processing is required	- Security risk: data is readable since it all takes the same path - Long delay if the line is broken as all data has to be rerouted - Nodes cannot undergo more than one communication at once - The line cannot be used by any other nodes
Packet switching	- Routes do not have to be reserved; multiple connections can occur at once - No security risk: data cannot be read since packets will take different routes - Less packets have to be re-requested if part of the line is broken	- Some packets may not arrive on time if they take a longer route between nodes - More processing is required to label each individual packet with the relevant details (order number, destination IP/MAC addresses, etc.)

Client-server vs peer-to-peer network topologies

- Client-server networks:
    o Clients and servers coexist on a network
    o Servers are computers that provide services (e.g. email, file storage, web access) to the clients on the network
    o The clients are the workstations connected to the network; they rely on the servers for the services they provide
- Peer-to-peer networks:
    o Client devices are connected without any central server in between
    o Hence file sharing is possible between two devices without having to store the files on a server
    o Multiple devices can contribute to the sending of files to increase speed and efficiency (torrenting)
    o All users on the network have equal allowances
    o Connections only need to be established when two nodes need to communicate

	Advantages	Disadvantages
Client-server networks	- Files stored centrally; not lost if a particular device breaks - Network peripherals, security and backups are centrally controlled and shared across devices - Users can access centrally-controlled shared data	- Specialist network operating system required - Servers are expensive to purchase - Specialist staff required to maintain network (network manager/s) - Large amounts of disruption caused if part of the network fails (e.g. broken file storage servers may cause large numbers of people to lose their files)
Peer-to-peer networks	- Torrenting reduces the load on individual devices when a large file is requested (e.g. for companies that want to share live video to large numbers of people) - No reliance on an individual server to store data; users are responsible for their own data on their own devices - No need for an operating system or servers to be maintained - Specialist staff not permanently required - Much easier to set up; requires less specialist knowledge - One computer failing will not disrupt other parts of the network unless it holds files that other members require	- Services such as printing have to be configured for each individual device since there is no server to maintain such connections - Data cannot be backed up centrally - Difficult to locate specific files without a logical filing system - Each user is responsible for making sure viruses are not introduced to the network - Little security since all users have the same permissions

Comparison essay questions are likely: make sure you can compare the two!

The internet relies on a variety of different technologies in order to be able to function effectively.

HTML elements:

```
<html>      defines a HTML document
<link>        defines the relationship between the document and an external resource (typically CSS)
<head>      defines information about the document
<title>     defines a title for the document
<body>     defines the document's body, where the main page content goes
<h1>          defines a large heading
<h2>         defines a moderately large heading
<h3>          defines a smaller heading
src            links to the imagine within the <img> tags
alt           provides a description of the image within the <img> tags
height    defines the height of an image within the <img> tags
width    defines the width of an imagine within the <img> tags
<div>       defines a section within the document
<form>      defines a form for user input on the webpage
<input>     defines an input control, where a user can enter data
<p>              defines a new paragraph
<li>          defines one bullet within a list
<ol>          defines an ordered (numbered) list
<ul>          defines an unordered list
<script>     defines a client-side script (JavaScript)
<img src="x" alt="y">   defines an image where x is the file and y is a description of the image
<a href="link">  defines a hyperlink where link  is the URL
```

CSS elements:

```
style                       used within elements in HTML to establish their properties, e.g.<h1style="color:blue;">
background-color     establishes the background colour behind the specified elements
border-color           establishes the colour of all borders surrounding the specified elements
border-style           establishes the style of all borders surrounding the specified elements
background-color     establishes the background colour behind the specified elements
border-width           establishes the width of all borders surrounding the specified elements
background-color     establishes the background colour behind the specified elements
color:a colour      establishes the colour of the specified elements
color:#XXXXXX      establishes the HEX colour of the specified elements
font-family         establishes the text font of the specified elements
font-size           establishes the text font size of the specified elements
height              establishes the height of the specified elements
width                establishes the width of the specified elements
#ID_name{   }       is used to define CSS for all HTML elements with the specified identifier
.class_name{   }     is used to define CSS for all HTML elements with the specified class
element{   }         is used to define CSS for all HTML elements of the specified type
```

Using JavaScript:

JavaScript uses the <script> tag and includes the following elements:

- `alert("Hello, world!");` will output the text "Hello, world!" in an alert window
- `document.write("Hello, world!");` will write the text "Hello, world!" into the object "document", assuming this is possible
- `var x = document.getElementById("myHeader");` declares a variable "x", which gets the value of "myHeader" from "document" (the HTML file)
- ```
  function myFunction() {
    document.getElementById("demo").innerHTML = "Paragraph changed!";
  }
  ```
  declares a function "myFunction" that changes the value of "demo" within the HTML to "Paragraph changed!" using the innerHTML property
  ```

File compression: reducing the size of a file so it occupies less space on a storage medium

- Either uses **utility software** or applications that **provide compressed output formats** (e.g. Photoshop can convert .png to .jpg)

  Advantages:
  - ✓ More space allows you to <u>store more files</u> on the storage medium
  - ✓ Smaller files are <u>faster to send/receive</u>, particularly with low bandwidth

  Disadvantages:
  - ✗ Processing resources are required to decompress files
  - ✗ Duplicates are created during decompression; this reduces the usefulness of the process when you have low disk space
  - ✗ Often dependant on software when receiving/archiving (e.g. WinRAR to unzip .rar files)

Lossy compression:

- **Quality is affected – data is lost**
- Final quality is dependent on the level of compression
- Takes a series of close-together values and approximates them to a single value (e.g. multiple similar pixels in an image become one colour)
- Used when the original quality is unnecessary or when bandwidth/disk space is the primary concern
- Has a better compression ratio, compared to lossless, since more data is lost
- E.g. JPEG files use lossy compression to allow the user to compromise between size and quality

Before lossy compression	After lossy compression

Lossless compression:

- **Quality is unaffected – no data is lost**
- All original data is readable after compression/decompression
- Used when the data being archived is important (e.g. letters such as bank statements, important raw photos, program files, etc.)

May use an LZ/LZW dictionary-based compression algorithm:

- Created a 'dictionary' of repeated code
- Assigns the code in the dictionary a shorter, unique key
- This key replaces all instances of the code within the file
- E.g.:

> Be prepared to compare lossy and lossless!

Old MacDonald had a farm
E-I-E-I-O
And on his farm he had a cow
E-I-E-I-O
With a moo moo here
And a moo moo there
Here a moo, there a moo
Everywhere a moo moo
Old MacDonald had a farm
E-I-E-I-O

```
                    2
                    1
      And on his farm he had a cow
                    1
                With3here
                And3there
              Here4, there4
              Everywhere3
                    2
                    1
```

<u>Dictionary</u>

1 = "E-I-E-I-O"
2 ="Old MacDonald had a farm"
3 = " a moo moo "
4 = " a moo "

Data can exist in several different forms. This chapter covers the more basic data types and introduces the idea of binary addition and subtraction (joy...).

Primitive data types: the most basic forms of data within programming languages, used for data manipulation

- <u>Integer</u>: a whole number (positive or negative)
- <u>Real</u>: a number that can contain a decimal part (its accuracy is limited by the memory available to it)
- <u>Floating point</u>: a form of real numbers containing a mantissa and exponent as a compromise between range and precision
- <u>Character (char)</u>: a single Unicode character
- <u>String</u>: a set of pieces of data (generally used to hold multiple characters, i.e. words) – strings are sometimes thought of as arrays of chars
- <u>Boolean</u>: has two values: TRUE or FALSE

Positive integers in binary:

- Base 2; each digit column is 2x the value of the previous, where the rightmost digit (or the one before the decimal point) represents the value 1
- Subscript $_2$ or $_b$ is used to signify that it's binary

Column value	512	256	128	64	32	16	8	4	2	1	.	1/2	1/4	1/8
Example 1	0	0	0	0	1	0	0	1	0	1	.	0	0	0
Example 2	0	0	0	0	0	1	0	1	1	0	.	0	1	1

= 132 + 4 + 1 = 37

= 16 + 4 + 2 + 1/4 + 1/8 = 22.375

Sign and Magnitude binary:

- The leftmost digit determines whether the number is positive or negative (0 = positive, 1 = negative)
- The rest of the digits are treated as normal
- $10111010_2 = -(2 + 8 + 16 + 32) = -58$
- $00111010_2 = 2 + 8 + 16 + 32 = 58$

> **Most significant bit** = the bit on the far left (holds the most value)
> **Least significant bit** = the bit on the far right (holds the least value)

Two's Compliment binary:

- The leftmost value is negative
- $10111010_2 = -128 + 2 + 8 + 16 + 32 = -70$
- $00111010_2 = 2 + 8 + 16 + 32 = 58$

Addition of binary numbers:

- 0 + 1 = 0 1
- 1 + 1 = 1 0
- 1 + 1 + 1 = 1 1
- 1 + 1 + 1 + 1 = 1 0 0

It's best to practise binary addition/subtraction – there's a high chance it'll come up in the exams.

Subtraction of binary numbers:

- 1 - 0 = 1
- 1 - 1 = 0
- For 0 - 1, a 1 can be 'borrowed' from a column further along (see below)

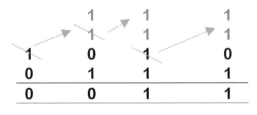

1) A 2 (a 1 from the 2nd column) is split into two 1s (in the 1st column). (1+1)-1 = 1.
2) Since the second column is now 0 - 1, the 8 (4th column) is split into two 4s (3rd column), and one of the new 4s is split into two 2s (2nd column). (1+1)-1 = 1.
3) 1 – 1 = 0
4) 0 – 0 = 0

Hexadecimal:

- Base 16 (each digit column 16 x the value of the previous), again starting at 1
- Uses numbers 1-9, then A-F (A = 10, F = 15)
- $3E_{16} = (3 \times 16) + 14 = 62$

Converting from 8-bit binary to hexadecimal:

1. Split the binary into two 'nibbles' (4-bit sections)
2. Each 'nibble' corresponds to each hexadecimal digit

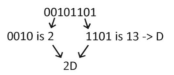

Normalised floating point:

- Floating point numbers consist of a mantissa and an exponent, representing a number in the form: mantissa x $2^{exponent}$
- The length of the mantissa and exponent will always be specified
- All floating point numbers are written in two's compliment
- The mantissa and/or the exponent can be negative
- If more bits are needed than are available, the least significant bits are discarded, since they hold the least value, and the value is rounded
- Normalisation is the storing of numbers in the most accurate and resourceful way without any unnecessary bits
- The rules of normalisation:
    - Positive mantissas start with 01
    - Negative mantissas start with 10
    - A binary point is implied after the 1st digit
- You may have to convert binary values to normalised floating point – practise!

Character sets:

- Sets of symbols (letters, numbers, etc.) that are assigned numerical values (denary, binary, hexadecimal, etc.) that can be interpreted within machine code
- Some character sets can cater for multiple languages (thus more people), at the expense of being larger (using more memory) and requiring more bits per symbol – an example of such a character set is UNICODE
- Note: lowercase letters will have different character set codes to their uppercase equivalents
- For example, the word JOHN in ASCII looks like this:
  01001010 01001111 01001000 01001110
- ASCII and UNICODE use 8 and 16 bits per character respectively

Character sets of computers:

- Normally equate to the symbols on a keyboard
- These characters can be understood/interpreted by the computer
- May include control characters (e.g. backspace)

UNICODE:

- A character set that aims to assign a unique code to all of the characters throughout the world
- These characters come from different languages and platforms
- UNICODE is not a fixed size: it continues to grow and currently contains over 100,000 characters
- Uses 16 bits per character

> You may be expected to know the decimal values of A-Z/a-z characters in ASCII/UNICODE. The simplest way of doing this is to learn the A/a values and count ahead.
>
> For ASCII and UNICODE, 65 = A, 97 = a and 48 = 0
>
> You may notice that, in binary, A is 0100 0001, B is 0100 0010.
> This means the position in the alphabet is the **binary value with the value 64 removed**
>
> 0100 0010 -> 0000 0010 -> B
>
> Similarly, for lower-case values, the position in the alphabet is **binary value with the values 64 and 32 removed.**
>
> 0110 0010 -> 0000 0010 -> b

Programs need to temporarily store data in different ways, depending on their purpose. Make sure you understand the key differences between the different data structures and their uses.

An array is:

- A data structure with a fixed length
- Stores multiple values of the same data type
- The values are grouped under a single identifier (the name of the array)
- Elements in the array can be accessed using their 'index'

  ```
  int[] nums = new int[5];
  ```
  This declares (in Java) an array, length 5, of integers. The array's identifier is nums.

  ```
  int[] nums = new int[]{1, 4, 5, 6, 7};
  ```
  This declares an array containing the integers 1, 4, 5, 6 and 7. The length is 5, since 5 integers were entered

  Arrays in Java:

  - Each value within the array is accessed via its index
  - For the example above, `nums[0]` would return 1 (**zero-based indexing applies; the number 1 is position zero**)
  - `nums.length` returns the length of the array; note that there are no parentheses as there are with Strings
  - Assignment statements can be used to assign values to elements within the array using their indexes; `nums[4]= 24;` would replace the value 7 at `nums[4]` with 24
  - Note that the last value in the array is always `nums[nums.length-1]`

  Arrays of multiple dimensions:

  - 2D or 3D arrays are simply arrays that contain arrays
    ```
    int[][] nums = new int[10][10];
    ```
  - The code above declares a 2D array called nums
  - The array contains 10 further arrays, each containing 10 integers
  - For example:
    - `nums[4]` is the 5th array within nums
    - `nums[4][0]` is the first value within the 5th array within nums

    If you only declare the length of an array, its values are initialized automatically:
  - Ints are set to 0
  - Strings are set to "" (empty)
  - Booleans are set to FALSE

Records:

- Each record corresponds to a row in a table and to a unique entity
- Consists of fields/attributes (that may have different datatypes) that state values related to/describing the entity
- E.g. a customer has a surname, first name, address, etc.
- See Databases – page 23

Lists:

- A collection sorting an ordered sequence of elements
- Each element is accessible via an index
- Each list has a size: the number of elements that have been added
- Elements can be added anywhere (front, back, in between two other elements)
- In Java, lists are represented as ArrayList objects
- Example of an ArrayList being used in Java:

```
ArrayList<String> name = new ArrayList<String>();
```

Index	0	1	2	3	4	5	6
Value	"cake"	"hello"	"joe"	"string"	"goose"	"halo"	"dog"

Function	Return type	Example	Return value	Description
.add	Void	`name.add("hello");` `name.add(3, "hello");`	N/A	Adds the specified element (to the end of the list if no index is given or otherwise to the specified index. Throws an exception if the index does not exist).
.clear	Void	`name.clear();`	N/A	Removes all elements in list.
.contains	Boolean	`name.contains("hello");`	TRUE	Determines whether specified element exists in the list.
.get	Object (String here)	`name.get(4);`	"goose"	Returns the element at the specified index (or throws an exception if the index does not exist).
.indexOf	Integer	`name.indexOf("hello");`	1	Returns the index of the specified value or -1 if not present in list.
.remove	Object	`list.remove(6);`	N/A	Removes the item at the specified index (or throws an exception if this index does not exist)
.set	Object	`list.set(4, "haha");`	N/A	Replaces the element at the specified index with the specified value (or throws an exception if the index does not exist).
.size	Integer	`list.size();`	7	Returns the number of elements in the list.

Tuples:

- Do not exist in Java but do in Python
- Another form of sequence
- The entire tuple (including its values) is defined and remains immutable (the elements cannot be changed)
- Only the whole tuple can be replaced by reassignment
- Supports the storing of multiple datatypes within the same tuple

```
01   #example of tuples in python
02   #notice how data types can be mixed
03   #unlike arrays and arraylists
04   tuple1 = ('computing', 'maths', 22);
05   tuple2 = (1, 2, 3, 4, 5, 6, 7, 8);
06   tuple3 = ("a", "b", 42, 91);
07
08   #accessing values in tuples
09
10   print tuple1[0];
11   #output -> computing
12   print tuple2[1:5];
13   #output -> [2, 3, 4, 5]
14
15   #deleting a tuple
16   del tuple1;
```

Stacks:

- Stacks are a **LIFO (Last In, First Out)** data structure
- Hence, elements are removed from a stack in the reverse order to being inserted
- **Selective removal operations** are not possible – only the item at the front of the stack is accessible
- Stacks can be modelled using arrays
- **One pointer** is used to point to the next avaliable free space in the stack
- Hence, if a new item is added, the pointer is incremented
- If the pointer is equal to the **length of the stack**, the stack must be full
- If the pointer is equal to **zero**, the stack must be empty
- See page 62 for more on stacks
- An example of a stack in use is the **call stack**:
    - Controls the way procedures and functions call, return and pass parameters to each other - a LIFO (Last In, First Out) data structure
    - Keeps track of return addresses to update program counter
    - Allows parameters to be passed and hence data to be transferred between functions/procedures
    - Holds local variables of each function/procedure and removes them when the function/procedure completes

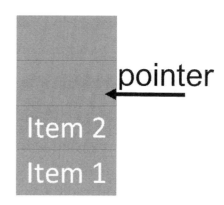

Queues:

- Queues are **FIFO (First In, First Out)** data structures
- Hence, elements are removed from a queue in the same order they're inserted
- Items are **added to the rear** of the queue and **retrieved from the front** of the queue
- Two pointers are used to point to the front of the queue (the position of the next item to be removed) and the rear of the queue (the position in which the next entry is to be placed)
- See page 62 for a list of operations on queues

The operations used to add/remove items to/from queues are on page 62 – you may need to use them in your algorithms during the exams!

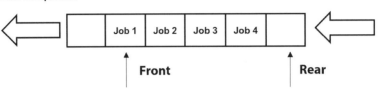

Front   **Rear**

- Forms of implementation of queues:
  - o Linear queues:

	0	1	2	3	4	5
			Rob	Sam	Lisa	Anna

- ▪ Linear queues can fill very quickly, since new data is only ever added at the end
- ▪ Hence, when items at the start are removed (see above), this space will never be refilled

  - o Circular queues:

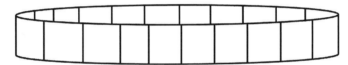

- ▪ Circular queues solve the above problem, since the queue no longer has a defined start and end
- ▪ Hence, if items at the front of the queue are removed, this space can be refilled once the end of the queue has looped around

- Uses of queues:
  - o Printer queues:
    - ▪ Outputs waiting to be printed can be stored in a queue
    - ▪ This is useful in networked environments, since items are printed in a first come, first served order
  - o Keyboard buffers:
    - ▪ Character inputs from a keyboard may be stored in a queue if the processor is busy
    - ▪ This ensures that the inputs are received and processed in the correct order
  - o Computer processes:
    - ▪ To hold jobs waiting to be processed by the computer (see Operating Systems)

Static vs Dynamic data structures:

- Static data structures cannot change their size whilst the program is running

    o For example, arrays in most programming languages cannot change their declared dimensions

- Dynamic data structures can increase and decrease in size whilst the program is running

	Advantages	Disadvantages
Static	- Easy to program - Easy to check for overflow - Compiler can allocate space when compiling the program - Often allows for random access (retrieving items from anywhere within the structure)	- Programmer has to estimate the maximum amount of space that will be required - Hence, a lot of space may be wasted
Dynamic	- Storage no longer needed can be returned to the system for use elsewhere - Uses only what's needed at any time (efficient use of memory)	- Harder to program - Can be slower to implement searching the data structure

Boolean Logic gates:

NOT / Negation:
- Exam notation: Q=¬A
- Java notation: Q=!A

A	Q
0	1
1	0

AND / Conjunction:
- Exam notation: Q=A^B
- Java notation: Q = A&&B

A	B	Q
0	0	0
0	1	0
1	0	0
1	1	1

OR / Disjunction:
- Exam notation: Q=AvB
- Java notation: Q=A||B

A	B	Q
0	0	0
0	1	1
1	0	1
1	1	1

XOR / Exclusive Disjunction:
- Exam notation: Q = A⊻B
- Java notation: Q=A^B

A	B	Q
0	0	0
0	1	1
1	0	1
1	1	0

Note: a circle attached to any of the other logic gates denotes the opposite of the gate's normal output.

E.g.

is the equivalent of

Order of operations:

Assignment	OR	AND	XOR	NOT	Parenthesis
=	||	&&	^	!	( )

last → *first*

Assignment	Add/Subtract	Multiply / Divide / MOD (remainder)	Parenthesis
=	+ -	* / %	( )

Boolean logic can be used to define problems:

Michel's house alarm needs to be set **at night** (N) or **from 8am – 8pm on weekdays** (W) or if she's not **at home** (H).

Using exam notation:
Q=NvWv¬H

Using a logic gate diagram:

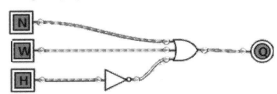

Karnaugh maps:

- Karnaugh maps are a graphical method of simplifying Boolean expressions
- Why do we simplify Boolean expressions?
    - Boolean logic is used in circuitry
    - Simplifying Boolean expressions reduces the number of logic gates (hardware) used
    - In turn, this reduces power consumption, cost, the chance of errors, interconnections, etc.

2-variable Karnaugh maps:

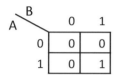

The table shows the possible results for A^B .
TRUE is only returned when A **and** B are TRUE.

4-variable Karnaugh maps:

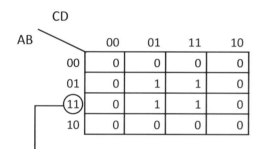

The table shows the possible results for B^D.
TRUE is only returned when B **and** D are TRUE.

A is TRUE (1), B is TRUE (1).
**NOTE: multiple-variable Karnaugh maps MUST be written in this order
(00, 01, 11, 10)**

Using Karnaugh maps to simplify expressions:

E.g.: (C^¬B)[∨] (C^¬A)[∨] (A^¬B ^C^¬D) [∨] (A^B^¬C) [∨](C^D^¬A)

1) Create and fill in a Karnaugh map:

CD

AB	00	01	11	10
00	0	0	1	1
01	0	0	1	1
11	1	1	0	0
10	0	0	1	1

2) Label all groups of 1s (TRUEs) that contain a 'power of 2' (i.e. groups of 2, 4, 8, etc.) and identify the rule for each group. **Groups can be across the edges** (e.g. a group of 4 could be made from all 4 corners if they were all TRUE), since they're technically all next to one another in a square. The groups **must be as large as possible** to simplify the expression fully - groups can overlap in order to make each group larger.

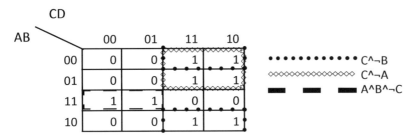

Therefore, the most simplified form of the expression is: (C^¬B)v(C^¬A)v(A^B^¬C) [the brackets aren't necessary because of the order of operations].

Boolean laws:
- A, B, C take either the value 1 or 0
- These laws are used to simplify Boolean expressions algebraically
- You don't need to remember the names of the laws, but it's useful to understand why the laws work

1. Law of Identity:
   - A=A
   - ¬A=¬A
2. Commutative Law:
   - A^B = B^A
   - AvB = BvA
3. Associative Law:
   - A^(B^C)=A^B^C
   - Av(BvC)=AvBvC
4. Idempotent Law:
   - A^A=A
   - AvA=A
5. Double Negative Law:
   - ¬(¬A)=A
6. Complementary Law:
   - A^(¬A)=0
   - Av(¬A)=1

7. Law of Intersection:
   - A^1=A
   - A^0=0
8. Law of Union:
   - Av1=1
   - Av0=A
9. DeMorgan's Theorem:
   - ¬(A^B)=(¬A)v(¬B)
   - ¬(AvB)=(¬A)^(¬B)
10. Distributive Law:
    - A^(BvC)=(A^B)v(A^C)
    - Av(B^C)=(AvB)^(AvC)
11. Law of Absorption:
    - A^(AvB)=A
    - Av(A^B)=A
12. Law of Common Identities:
    - A^(¬AvB)=A^B
    - Av(¬A^B)=AvB

It's important that you're familiar with the following acts and how they can be applied to various scenarios. It may be useful to add your own notes, perhaps including recent news articles related to the acts.

The Data Protection Act 1998:

The Data Protection Act is designed to protect the privacy of data:
- Customers have the right to see the data and ask for it to be changed if incorrect so they aren't responsible for incorrect data
- Data must be lawfully collected to obey customers' rights
- Data can only be accessed/altered by authorised individuals to prevent malicious changes
- Such authorised people must be notified to the Data Protection Register so they are accountable
- Data should only be used for its **specified** purpose; this deters junk mail
- Data collection should not be excessive; only relevant data should be stored
- Data should be accurate and up to date so that customers are not wrongly accused of wrongdoing
- Data should not be kept for any longer than necessary to allow customers to leave an organisation
- Data should be protected with adequate security measures to prevent malicious access and alteration
- Data should not be transferred out of the EU; this ensures it remains controlled by the Data Protection Act

Limitations:
- It can be difficult to monitor whether companies are abiding by the act
- Some parts of the world may not comply with this law; this makes it complicated to transfer data internationally
- The constant changing of technology means that the act must undergo constant review

The Copyright, Designs and Patents Act 1988:

The Copyright, Designs and Patents Act has two main purposes:
1) To ensure people are rewarded for their endeavours
2) To give protection to the copyright holder if someone tries to steal of copy their work

Examples of copying work in Computer Science may include:
- Copying/downloading music
- Copying software   } *Intellectual property*
- Copying images from the internet
- Copying text from webpage and using it in your work/pretending it is yours

Software licenses grant permission to a specified number of users to use software that they don't own themselves; these may be *single-user*, *multi-user* or *site licenses*

The Regulation of Investigatory Powers Act 2000:

The Regulation of Investigatory Powers Act 2000 is designed to:
- Provide a legal framework allowing organisations including the police and security services to carry out surveillance and access communications of all types between individuals
- Make it a crime to carry out surveillance or monitoring of communications if not authorised under the Act
- The ability for organisations to intercept communications was designed to:
    o Prevent/detect crimes
    o Prevent public disorder
    o Ensure national security and the safety of the general public
    o Investigate or detect illegal use of telecommunication systems
- Some organisations monitor the websites that employees visit in order to ensure that staff time is being used effectively
- Some employees argue that this is a breach of trust and an invasion of privacy

Misuse of the Act:
- The number of organisations able to intercept communications has risen from an initial 9 to around 1000
- Hence, many people consider the Act excessive and a threat to privacy
- Some are concerned that the Act is being abused in order to monitor things beyond what was originally intended

Encryption:
- If held data is encrypted, the Act can be used to force individuals to surrender encryption keys to allow the data to be accessed
- Refusing can result in up to two years in prison

The Computer Misuse Act 1990:

The Computer Misuse Act recognised the following new offences:
1. Unauthorised access to computer material
    - The lowest level of offence
    - Includes any form of accessing material that is not rightfully yours
    - Up to six months in prison and/or a hefty fine

Unauthorised access with intent to commit/facilitate a crime
    - As for the above, but doing so with the intent of doing something illegal
    - E.g. accessing someone's bank account
    - Up to five years in prison and/or a hefty fine
2. Unauthorised modification of computer material
    - The deletion or modification of files with the intent of causing damage to an individual or company
    - This includes purposely introducing a virus to a system
    - Up to five years in prison and/or a fine
3A. Making/supplying/obtaining anything which could be used for computer misuse
    - Making: the creation of malicious software such as viruses, malware, etc.
    - Supplying: distribution of any of the above material, regardless of how it was obtained
    - Obtaining: purposely obtaining any of the above material that you know could be used to damage a computer system

Limitations:
- It can be difficult to prove that there was intent; many say they weren't aware of the implications of their actions or that they possessed malicious software; hence, there are very few prosecutions
- It can be very easy to break the law in this way, which supports the argument above
- People with technical knowledge are likely to be able to 'cover their tracks'
- It can be difficult to trace who was responsible for the offence; some claim that someone else accessed their account to commit the offence
- The damage to the system is usually complete once the offender is caught; this damage is usually irreversible (e.g. losing, damaging or leaking data)

Seriousness

1.5.2 - Ethical, moral and cultural issues

Make sure you're able to discuss the pros and cons of the following topics in relation to different scenarios. You will be likely to have an essay-based question in the exam that encompasses an issue related to these topics. Add your own notes and practise talking about them.

- Computers in the workforce:
    - ✓ Faster, easier communication with other employees
    - ✓ Organisation: different types of software can organise documents, schedules and deadlines, leading to better time management and thus productivity
    - ✓ Ability to store much larger amounts of data than physically
    - ✓ Self-sufficiency; less need to rely on others since applications allow employees to do tasks that they would otherwise have needed to outsource
    - ✓ Can be used to do tasks that humans struggle with (e.g. assembling cars, rolling sheet metals, etc.)
    - ✗ Reduced communication skills; it can be harder to communicate via typed communications compared to face-to-face conversation
    - ✗ Increased stress to become computer literate, particularly on older or less-educated employees
    - ✗ Distractions (every three minutes, according to CNET News) due to emails, instant messages, phone calls, social media, etc. reduce productivity
    - ✗ Employees may feel disconnected from their work and their peers since more of their work is done electronically and thus involves less interaction
    - ✗ Employees may find it more stressful knowing that their work is being electronically monitored; such employees have less privacy
    - ✗ Heath issues: visual and musculoskeletal problems can develop from frequent use of computers

- Automated decision making:
    - ✓ Designed to imitate the decision a human would make in a situation
    - ✓ Relieves pressure from managers and professionals when difficult decisions need to be made
    - ✓ Allows decisions to be made without bias, meaning an individual cannot be blamed for mistakes
    - ✓ Can be used to reduce labour costs, enforce policies and respond more quickly to customers
    - ✗ Is not always necessary; 'a solution looking for a problem'
    - ✗ It can be difficult to place trust in a machine to make a decision that has a large effect/affects a large number of people
    - ✗ People may consider it unfair if a computer makes a decision that they don't agree with
    - ✗ People may lose their jobs as technology replaces their individual roles

- Environmental effects:
    - ✓ Technology can be used to improve medicine and thus healthcare
    - ✓ Hardware is often reusable
    - ✗ The use of technology drastically increases electricity usage and thus the requirement for energy generation
    - ✗ Electronic waste can be difficult to dispose of and some machines introduce toxic chemicals
    - ✗ It can be difficult to recycle hardware since technology is constantly changing and hence old hardware quickly becomes outdated

- Artificial intelligence:
    - ✓ Allows tasks to be performed more quickly
    - ✓ Allows tasks to be performed without/with less error
    - ✓ Computers do not experience pressure, nervousness, etc.
    - ✓ Can be used to aid humans in everyday tasks
    - ✓ Can be used to help eradicate war, disease and poverty
    - ✗ AI could be programmed to do something devastating
    - ✗ AI could be programmed to do something beneficial, but may develop a destructive way of achieving this goal
    - ✗ AI could become more powerful than humans; if they became destructive, they would be very difficult to stop

- Censorship and the Internet:
    - ✓ Internet censorship provides the ability to let vulnerable people (e.g. children) access the internet safely by blocking access to unsuitable content
    - ✓ Censorship allows the reduction of cybercrime by blocking access to illegal websites
    - ✗ A lack of censorship can lead to people being taken advantage of or influenced by content unsuitable to them (e.g. the extremist group ISIS used the internet to recruit vulnerable people from foreign countries)
    - ✗ Governments may take advantage of their ability to censor content on the internet to silence opposition or otherwise control their citizens
    - ✗ Some believe that any form of censorship is wrong, as access to knowledge is a human right

- Monitor behaviour:
    - ✓ Monitoring customers' use of the internet allows companies to better tailor adverts and content to their users: for example, you may see adverts for products related to your previous browsing history
    - ✓ Governments' monitoring of citizens can be used to maintain national security by finding information on, for example, suspected terror attacks
    - ✗ Companies often try to hide the fact that they are collecting data on customers
    - ✗ Many customers may consider this to be an intrusion into their privacy

- Analyse personal information:
    - ✓ Similar to the above, people's daily lives can be monitored to allow companies to tailor themselves to individuals; for example, the things you buy with a membership card may affect the adverts you're sent – many customers find this useful
    - ✓ The monitoring of private communications can again be used to detect criminal activity
    - ✗ Many, again, consider this an intrusion into their privacy

- Piracy and offensive communications:
    - ✗ Piracy is very easy to commit due to digital technology – it's very easy to share copyrighted content online; as a result, many commit such crimes unintentionally or simply do not consider it an offence but are still liable to prosecution under The Copyright, Designs and Patents Act
    - ✗ Many content creators lose recognition and money due to piracy of their content

- Layout, colour paradigms and character sets:
    - ✓ People can tailor the styles of their websites based on their cultures and target audience
    - ✓ This can include building websites with layouts that may change depending on the countries of visitors
    - ✗ Different cultures tend to interpret different styles in different ways; this runs the risk of people being offended or finding it difficult to understand a website that isn't suited to them

2.1.1 – Thinking abstractly

What is abstraction?

- In Computer Science, abstraction is used to simplify problems or ideas into abstract models
- All unnecessary detail is removed so that only relevant information is seen
- This makes the problem or idea easier to understand and use
- Parts of the problem or idea may be grouped into similar categories or abstraction layers – this is used during stepwise refinement (see page 51) and the TCP/IP model (page 30)
- Abstraction layers help to represent a solution as a series of stages that can be followed

- A flat shape
- Four sides
- Each side is straight
- All sides have equal length
- Each interior angle is a right angle
- Is a quadrilateral
- Is a polygon

- Square

2.1.2 – Thinking ahead

The ability to think ahead includes the following:
- Identifying the inputs and outputs of a system (see page 8)
- Considering the preconditions necessary for solving problems (a basic example would be declaring a tracking variable before use in a WHILE loop)
- Identifying when parts of a system can be reused (e.g. using libraries to reuse software)
- Considering possible errors when building a system and taking the necessary action to prevent them
- Considering how a user's requirements may change
- Making a system flexible so that changes can be easily implemented if the user's requirements are likely to change

2.1.3 – Thinking procedurally

Thinking procedurally includes the following:
- Being able to break down a problem using stepwise refinement as a form of abstraction into individual components
- Identifying the parts of a system that will be regularly used and partitioning them into reusable modules
- Considering the parameters that reusable modules will take and ensuring their suitability
- Considering the order of the steps required to solve a problem

2.1.4 – Thinking logically

Finally, thinking logically involves the following skills:
- Identifying where decisions need to be made within programs
- Considering the conditions that affect the outcomes of these decisions
- Considering how the outcomes of these decisions affect flow through the program

Three programming constructs:

1 - Sequence:
- The order in which statements are executed
- All instructions are executed, once, in the order in which they appear

```
int x = 2;
int y = 3;
int z  = x * y
```

2 - Iteration:
- A group of instructions are repeated, either **a set number of times** or **until a condition is/isn't met**
- The most common form of iteration is a loop:
- FOR loop:
  - Repeats **a set number of times**
  - Uses a 'tracking variable' that's incremented after each loop
  - The code below will repeat until the condition (i < 10) is **no longer met** (10 times)
  - The condition is evaluated at the **beginning** of the loop

```
for(int i = 0; i < 10; i++){
        System.out.println("i is less than 10"); }
```

- WHILE loop:
  - Repeats **until a condition is no longer met**
  - Uses a tracking variable that's declared outside of the loop and incremented after each loop
  - The condition is evaluated at the beginning of the loop

```
int i = 4;
while(i > 2){
        System.out.print(i);
        i = i + 1; }
```

- REPEAT loop:
  - Repeats **until a condition is met**
  - Uses a tracking variable that's declared outside of the loop
  - The condition is evaluated at the **end of the loop**
  - The REPEAT loop <u>does not exist in Java</u>, but looks like this in exam pseudocode:

```
int i = 4
REPEAT
    i = i + 1
    output i
UNTIL i < 4
```

3 - Branching:
- Branching is when code causes the computer to deviate from its normal sequence of execution by beginning the execution of a different sequence of instructions
- E.g. function calls: a new section of code is executed within the current section

```
int x = 4
int y = sqrt(x)
```

Variables: global scope:

- A variable is defined at the start of the program and visible throughout the entire program
- Only used when a value may need to be accessed by multiple parts of a program (e.g. an exchange rate)
- Allows modules to share data
- Should be avoided where possible:
  - Global variables make it harder to integrate modules
  - Modules are no longer independent if they rely on the same global variable, hence increasing the complexity of the program
  - May cause conflicts with other variables in other parts of the program (e.g. with the same name)
  - May be changed accidently or unexpectedly in complex programs
  - Errors with the variable can be harder to trace since any of the modules could have changed its value

Variables: local scope:

- Defined within a construct (function, procedure, WHILE loop, etc.)
- Its use and visibility is restricted solely to that construct
- To make efficient use of memory, the variable is destroyed once the construct is completed
- Hence, the same variable identifier can be used in unrelated constructs since both cannot run at once

Modularity in programs and stepwise refinement:

- Program code is typically separated into individual 'modules' which can then be produced by different people within a team
- Stepwise refinement is a form of problem solving in which a large task is continuously broken down into several smaller sub-tasks until they are small enough to be coded
- Each task is defined in simple terms
- Programs to be written are broken down into smaller modules to be solved using stepwise refinement
- The individual modules are determined using a top-down design diagram:

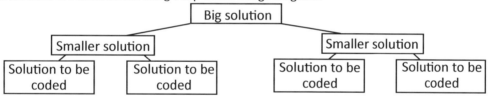

- The individual modules are called **nodes**; leaf nodes are those at the ends of the branches (the smallest form of the problems)
- This top-down design generally perpetuates a modular form of development (modules are designed and built separately and combined at the end to form the overall solution)
- Advantages:
  - Different programmers can work on the modules most suited to their individual skill sets
  - The program will, hence, be completed more quickly
  - Debugging will be carried out on small sections of code, hence reducing the likelihood of errors and their severity
  - Smaller modules allow for more thorough testing
  - Library routines can be used and existing modules can be referenced in new code, saving programming time and space
  - It is easy to swap one module for another if modifications are needed
  - Completion of the overall program is easier to monitor since the design is better structured

Functions vs procedures:

Functions:
- A section of a program with a unique identifier that performs a specific task
- Returns a single value
- Generally takes parameters
- Used as part of an expression; often called an inline

  e.g. `int x = sqrt(4);`

  `sqrt()` is the function in this case

Procedures:
- Also a sub-section of code with a unique identifier that performs a specific task
- Does not usually return a value; returns values by reference if so
- Used as an instruction/statement

  e.g. `resetHighScores()`

Passing by value:

- The <u>values</u> of variables are used as parameters for a function and are stored under a different identifier within the function
- Hence, the variables themselves will not be altered unless the function alters them specifically

```
int x = 3;
doSomething(x)


FUNCTION doSomething (int q byVal)
{
      q = 4
}
/* the value of x will not change */
```

Passing by reference:
- References to the variables are used as parameters for a function
- Altering the values of the references will change the value of the original variable

```
int x = 3;
doSomething(x)


FUNCTION doSomething (int q byRef)
{
      q = 4
}
/* the value of x will change */
```

Types of error:

Syntax errors:
- Misspellings of reserved words (e.g. `retrun` or `Return` instead of `return`)
- An error in the rules of the language
- Writing a program instruction incorrectly

Logic/Semantic errors:
- An error in the logic of the algorithm
- Recognized when the program does not produce the desired output (during testing)
- Some IDEs can recognize simple logic errors (e.g. `IF(maybe = TRUE)` instead of `IF(maybe == TRUE))`

Run time/Arithmetic:
- Attempting to perform an arithmetic operation that cannot be done (e.g. dividing by zero)
- This will cause the program to crash
- Stack overflow – recursive code means too many return addresses are placed on the call stack
- Library errors – referring to a library routine/function that does not exist

Integrated Development Environments (IDEs):

-   A single program that's used to develop other programs
-   Consists of a number of different components that deal with different aspects of development

Debugging techniques provided by IDEs:

-   <u>Translator diagnostics</u>
    -   o   Provide information on syntax errors or logic errors such as calling non-existent variables
    -   o   Shows where the error occurred and gives an indication of the error made
-   <u>Break points</u>
    -   o   Allows software execution to be stopped/paused on a particular line, where the values of variables can be observed
-   <u>Single stepping</u>
    -   o   Allows line-by-line execution of the program, controlled by the user, to inspect how the values of variables change
    -   o   Helps errors to be located within the program (e.g. when a variable's value changes to something unexpected/unexpectedly)
    -   o   Can help new programmers understand the logic of an algorithm that was written by someone else
-   <u>Watch and trace</u>
    -   o   Outputs the values of all existing variables when using single stepping
-   <u>Variable inspection/dump</u>
    -   o   Studying the values of variables at a certain point within the code (e.g. at breakpoints)
-   <u>Cross references</u>
    -   o   Identifies where variables are used within the program to help determine if two variables have been assigned the same name
-   <u>Crash dumps</u>
    -   o   Outputs variable values and the contents of the call stack at the point where an error occurs

- It's important to be familiar with the general way in which software is designed and developed - this is often referred to as the System Development Life Cycle (SDLC)

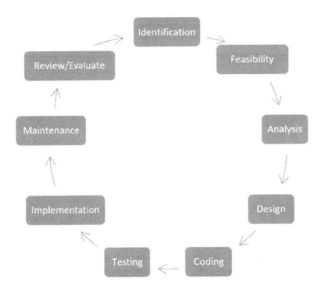

1) Identification:
   - The clients' problems/user requirements are **accurately** identified through an extensive interview
   - The developers and clients must ensure they have the **same interpretation of the desired outcome**

2) Feasibility study:
   - Checks if there's an actual need for the project/whether it's possible
   - Is it technically feasible?
   - Is it economically feasible?
   - Is it legal?
   - Is the end user capable of running the new system?
   - Is the budget sufficient to cover the expected development costs?
   - Is the solution socially acceptable?
   - Is development of the system possible in the given time period?

3) Analysis:
   - Identifies the information requirements of the system
   - Will generally use the old system (if there is one) as a guideline

   Areas to investigate:
   - Details of how the current system works
   - Inputs used in the current system and their desired outputs
   - How these inputs/outputs are processed
   - Data storage:
     - How data is accessed
     - How long data is stored for
     - The quantity of data stored
     - Data types
     - Forms of data storage
   - Users of the system:
     - Their roles
     - Their levels of experience and how they interact with one another
     - Hence, the types of system best suited to them
   - Hardware requirements

   Forms of analysis:
   - Interviews
   - Observations
   - Questionnaires/surveys
   - Meetings
   - Reviewing existing documents on the current system

4) <u>Design:</u> must **solve the specified problem**

Parts of the design:

- o Specification
- o UI
- o Specification of data structures
- o Prototyping
- o Algorithms
- o Hardware
- o Forms of inputs and their handling
- o Forms of outputs
- o Validation
- o Security of data
- o Data structures required to hold the data
- o The processing required to change inputs into acceptable outputs
- o Flow charts and data flow diagrams will often be used as a form of design (see below)

<u>Any software engineer should be able to create your software using your design.</u>

Prototyping:

- A simple version of a program is created to illustrate a feature of the system
- This will generally be input/output screens
- These screens are often dummies: they do not actually work
- Storyboards may be used to show how these screens link together
- Screens show the end users how the system will look, allowing issues to be identified and thus for the end user to be part of the design through feedback
- Helps to research new ideas

Flow charts:

- Shows how **processes** in the system start and end
- Shows the individual programs required to turn inputs into the desired outputs
- May specify the hardware required

Data flow diagrams:

- Shows the path of data through the system
- Shows where data comes from, the processing carried out and where the data moves to
- Show how this data is stored

5) <u>Building/Coding:</u>

How?

- o Which programming language? This varies depending on what's being produced
- o Where do we start? Which part of the program do we build first?
  - Modular design: different groups build/test individual components of the program that are later joined together

Standards and conventions:

- o The team must <u>agree</u> on the basic standards they use to write code (e.g. how they name variables, where code is commented, etc.)
- o This will generally be agreed through a group meeting

6) <u>Testing:</u>

- o More than simply 'does it work?'
- o There should be a strategic test plan in place to ensure the system functions in all ways required by the client
- o Testing is completed in planned stages, against the client's requirements
- o Each stage has its own plan
- o Each individual function is tested with extreme, normal and abnormal data (see page 58)
- o Ensures the system produces the desired outputs for particular inputs
- o See page 58 for more on testing

7) <u>Implementation:</u>

- o The stage during which the system is actually 'rolled out' and installed
- o This may include installing hardware and/or software and providing appropriate documentation

8) Maintenance:
   A. Adaptive: adds new features
      - Due to changes in the law
      - Due to changes in business needs
      - Due to changes in system processes
      - May require a payment
   B. Perfective: improves looks (aesthetical appeal) and performance
      - Refinement of user interface
      - Speed improvements
   C. Corrective: fixes existing problems/features that did not work
      - Bug fixes
      - Security patches

9) Review/evaluation:
   o Team must evaluate whether criteria has been met before they can be paid
   o Areas to evaluate:
   - Whether criteria were met
   - Performance; was the system fully tested?
      ▪ Black box, white box, acceptance testing
   - Usability of the system
   - Cost of producing system
   - Robustness of the system
      ▪ Security of data
      ▪ Reliability of system
   - Technical support provided
   - Maintainability of system

Examples of programming standards and their benefits:
- Short submodules (functions/procedures):
   o Forces algorithms to be simplified – reduces complexity
   o Easier to locate errors/debug
   o Readability; can be more easily understood by other programmers
   o Smaller submodules more likely to be able to be reused
   o Can be used with stepwise refinement (see page 51)
- Identifiers follow standard/agreed conventions:
   o E.g. camelCasing, meaningful identifiers
   o Readability; can be more easily understood by other programmers
   o Forces identifiers to explain the object in moderate detail to avoid identifier names being reused (duplication)
   o Makes maintenance of code easier
- Single entry points to submodules:
   o Reduces complexity of program
   o Easier to trace errors/debug
- Avoid hardware-specific code:
   o Prevents having to rewrite code/the entire program to suit different computer architectures
   o Maximises compatibility/portability across other architectures
- No/Few global variables:
   o Saves memory when program is running
   o Global variables have a dependency on other areas of the program
   o Reduces where to look for bugs
- Adequate documentation:
   o E.g. comments, meaningful identifiers
   o Source code hence easier to understand by others – readability/maintainability of program

Software development models:

1. Waterfall model:
   o Follows the same steps as the SDLC, in order
   o Each step produces information which influences the next stages
   o It may be necessary to return to previous stages to collect more information or check information that has been previously collected – the pure model would not allow this
   o If returning to a previous stage, all of the stages afterwards must be revisited
2. Agile:
   o More flexible; varies depending on the project and circumstances
   o Emphasis on communication and teamwork
   o Uses **sprints**: planned sections of time in which particular aspects of the system are analysed, designed, produced, tested and implemented into the overall system
   o Prototyping is likely during the early stages of sprints
   o More suited to small, short-term projects since long-term teamwork and face-to-face communication is much more difficult
   o The daily communication required to plan and review sprints can be time-consuming
3. Extreme programming (XP):
   o Similar to the agile model but designed to expect and adapt to large changes to the project during development
   o Emphasis on organising people to produce high-quality software more productively than other models
   o Aims to reduce costs in sudden changes to requirements by using multiple short development cycles in which the needs of the end-user are regularly considered
4. Spiral model:
   o The project is carried out as a series of loops
   o Each loop goes through most of the SDLC stages
   o Before each loop, a prototype is produced of some part of the system
   o Designed to manage risk and save money
   o **Iterative** cycle – multiple loops of the same stages take place in order to provoke improvement on the overall system
   o Once all of the stages in one 'loop' have been visited, an evaluation takes place before the stages are revisited
5. Rapid Application Development (RAD):
   o A prototype is designed with reduced functionality
   o The prototype is tested and evaluated with the end user in order to refine the next prototype
   o Each prototype has a set deadline
   o This process is repeated until the prototype is accepted by the end user and used to create a final product
   o This can be combined with the spiral model

	Advantages	Disadvantages
Waterfall	- Requirements are easily defined with the end user - Easy to identify progress - Stages can overlap to suit designers/builders	- Cannot go back if mistakes are made (as it's a one-way cycle); mid-project changes are difficult - Risky: end user won't see the project until testing begins
Agile	- High quality code (efficient) is produced that's constantly refactored	- Requires teamwork and collaboration - Requires an end-user (client) representative to be part of the team
Extreme programming (XP)	- No sudden high cost if the project undergoes a major change - Considers the needs of the end-users on a regular basis	- Difficult to plan effectively since changes to the project are to be expected -Often lacks the necessary structure documentation as a result of the above

Spiral	- Suitable for high-risk, larger projects with larger teams as risk is constantly assessed and managed - Easy to identify when problems arise and evaluate if it's worth moving forward	- Risk analysis is a separate, specialist skill, hence costing more money to hire an appropriate team member
RAD	- Prototypes produced quickly - Prototypes can be adapted through feedback from end user - Hence caters for rapidly-changing requirements - Useful when the user does not know 100% what they want - Emphasis on usability rather than coding efficiency	- Requires continual contact with end user - Not suitable for large projects when the teams are large - Constant changes can reduce code efficiency of what has already been created/may require code to be deleted

Stages of testing:
- o   Alpha:
    - 'In-house': done by the programmers in their offices
    - The programmer plays the role of the end user
    - Takes place during development in order to find bugs
- o   Beta:
    - The program is nearly complete
    - The program is given to a dedicated team or to potential end-users
    - Aims to identify bugs overlooked by the programmers
    - Tested as if in normal use (as intended)
- o   Acceptance/end user testing:
    - System given to the end user to prove that the program works correctly and meets the original requirements
    - Takes place before payment; user pays if satisfied
    - The program/system is considered complete
    - The program uses 'live' data (i.e. as part of the final system)

Test strategies:
- o   White box testing:
    - Ensures that all parts of the code itself function as intended
    - A programmer tests all possible steps through algorithms
    - Requires knowledge of the algorithm itself
- o   Black box testing:
    - A suitable set of inputs is tested against their desired outputs, without considering how the program actually works
    - Tests the functionality of the code; may not be performed by the programmers since it does not require knowledge of the algorithm itself

Forms of test data:
- Normal:
    - o   As would be normally inputted during use of the program
- Borderline:
    - o   Close to the borders between the different outputs produced (e.g. returning a library book the day before its due date)
- Extreme/Invalid:
    - o   Unlikely/Impossible test data (e.g. returning a library book in 704BC)

Algorithms are:

- A sequence of steps
- That are followed in a specified order
- That produce a desired effect (e.g. an output)

Bubble sort:

- A sorting algorithm (used to order an array)
- Each pair of items in the array is compared and swapped if the second is smaller than the first
- This continues until the end of the array is reached, at which point it starts at the beginning again
- Once the entire array has been searched and no changes have been made, the array must be in the right order and hence the sort is finished
- Requires multiple passes through the array
- Simple but inefficient and hence is rarely used
- Useful for reordering small numbers of items or an ordered list with a small number of errors
- Used to teach the processes of sorting algorithms but not practically useful on more than a small number of items
- **Pseudocode:**

```
FUNCTION bubbleSort (arrayName)
        int n = arrayName.length - 1
        Boolean swapped = true
        WHILE(swapped)
                swapped = false
                FOR(int i = 0; i < n, i++)
                        IF(arrayName[i] > arrayName[i+1])
                                int temp = arrayName[i]
                                arrayName[i] = arrayName[i+1]
                                arrayName[i+1] = temp          //swaps values
                                swapped = true
                        END IF
                END FOR
                n = n - 1     //Largest value always reaches end of array
        END WHILE             //so one less value needs to be considered
END FUNCTION                  //each time
```

Insertion sort:

- Builds the final sorted array one item at a time to the left of the unsorted values by inserting it into the correct position
- Requires only one pass through the array
- Compares a value in the array to the sorted array to the left – if smaller, the value is inserted into the sorted array; if larger, the value is already in the correct position (at the end of the sorted array)
- The running time depends on the initial order of the array – fast for large, partially-sorted arrays and small arrays but slower for randomly-ordered or reversed arrays
- Relatively simple to code
- Inefficient for large sets of values
- **Pseudocode:**

```
FUNCTION insertionSort(arrayName)
        FOR(int i = 1; i < arrayName.length; i++)
                int temp = arrayName[i]
                int n = i - 1
                WHILE(temp < arrayName[n])
                        arrayName[n+1] = arrayName[n]  //shuffles
                        n = n - 1                       //larger values
                END WHILE                               //forward once
                arrayName[n+1] = temp    //inserts temp into space
        END FOR
END FUNCTION
```

Linear searches:

- These are similar to serial searches in *file handling*
- Can be used on sorted or unsorted arrays
- More useful for **unsorted** arrays, since the required element could be **anywhere**
- o Compares every element in the array, starting from the beginning, to the given search key
- o If they are equal, the search is completed
- o Else, the search continues by moving to the next element
- o The search ends either when the given key is matched or until the end of the array is reached
- Pseudocode (for an array of integers):

```
FUNCTION search (int x)
   FOR(int i 0; i < arrayName.length; i++)
      IF (x = arrayName[i])
         return i;
      END IF
      return "error"   //if i has not been found, x does not exist in
END FUNCTION           //array and so error (or -1) should be returned
```

- NOTE: the purpose of this function is to find the **location** (index) of the specified integer x

Binary searches:

- - Can only be used on **sorted** arrays (e.g. an array of integers organised in ascending order)
- o Locates the middle of the array
- o Compares the value in the middle to the search key
- o If equal, the search is finished
- o Otherwise, decides which half of the array contains the search key
- o Discards the other half of the array
- o Repeats this process until the required key is found/there are no elements left to search

Index	0	1	2	3	4	5	6	7	8	9	10	11	12	13	14
Value	6	13	14	25	33	43	51	53	64	72	84	93	95	96	97

 low (0)   mid (7)   high (14)

- - This algorithm uses three variables to indicated the front, end and middle of the part of the array being searched
- - If, for example, you were searching for 33, the top half of the array would be discarded by making high = mid – 1 and then recalculating the middle of the new region
- - Pseudocode (for an array of integers):

```
FUNCTION search (int x)
      int high = arrayName.length - 1
      int low = 0
      WHILE(low <= high)  //ensures code repeats
          int mid = (low + high)/2
          IF (x > arrayName[mid])
              low = mid + 1
          ELSE IF (x < arrayName[mid])
              high = mid - 1
          ELSE
              return mid
          END IF
      END WHILE
      return -1/error
END FUNCTION
```

Linear vs Binary searches:

	Advantages	Disadvantages
Linear	- Easier to program - Can be used on both sorted and unsorted arrays	- Takes much longer to search (eliminates only one option per cycle)
Binary	- Much faster to search (as it eliminates half of all options per cycle)	- Requires the array to be sorted - More complex to program

Operations on stacks (see page 39):

- Adding to stacks:

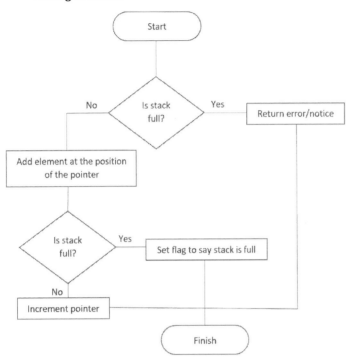

- Removing from stacks:

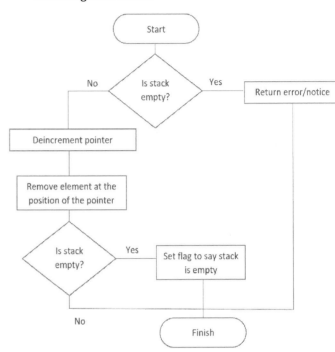

Operations on queues (see page 40):

- Adding to queues:

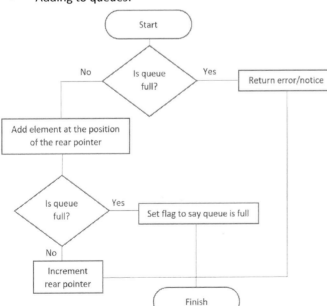

- Removing from queues

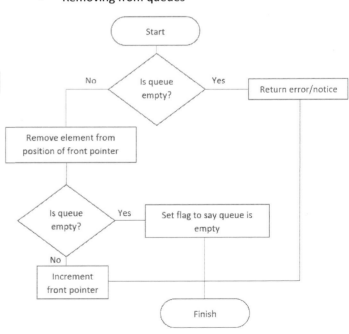

These algorithms are the same for circular
queues, except pointers are incremented using
position MOD (queue length) + 1

Printed in Great Britain
by Amazon